Pretty Patchwork Gifts

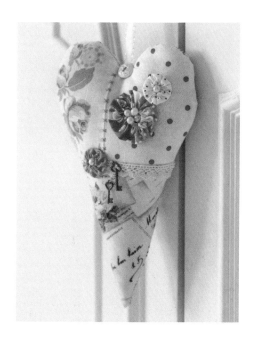

Helen Philipps

D&C
David and Charles

www.stitchcraftcreate.co.uk

Contents

With love to my dear friend, Ingrid

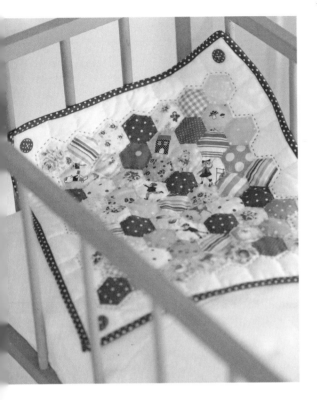

Introduction

Patchwork can be modern, fresh, contemporary, vintage, whimsical, subtle, bright, colourful, floral, or whatever you wish it to be. In this book I present my own take on making pretty patchwork projects, both for the home and as gifts, and each chapter features full instructions and illustrations in addition to templates and tips. I would like these ideas to be used as a starting point for your own interpretation and to inspire your own creativity.

For me, patchwork is about fabric, colour and pattern. It isn't just about making quilts; it's about creating smaller projects too and playing with leftover scraps of fabric to make something pretty to treasure. Patchwork can be used for making or decorating all kinds of items and this book has a tempting range of projects; from appliqué and log cabin cushions, hand-pieced doll's quilts, pretty birdhouses, brooches, boxes and bags to fabric sweets, flower garlands, dolls and even soft toy rabbits in pretty patched frocks.

I have always loved patchwork, ever since I discovered it in my school days from a friend's older sister. We made paper hexagons, covered them with fabric and pieced them together and from that moment I was hooked. Whatever other art and crafts I might be working on, I would always have a patchwork project going on as well. My interest in the craft has continued to grow year by year, especially as there are now so many wonderful quilting fabric ranges produced each season.

I hope you enjoy using this book, buying some gorgeous new fabrics and dipping into your stash to make something new and exciting and that you have a happy, crafty time whilst doing so.

Helen
x

Hearts and Flowers Cushion

This bright and fresh patchwork cushion is made using scraps of my favourite floral prints, which look so colourful and vibrant against the contrasting white patches. The appliqué hearts are so easy to create using simple templates and Bondaweb (iron-on interfacing). The cushion cover is an envelope type, where two pieces of fabric overlap at the centre of the cover along the length of the cushion back. You can have fun adding bold and unusual buttons to the back of the cushion as a little surprise for when it is turned over.

You will need

For the patchwork

- 18 pieces of assorted floral fabrics, 7.5cm (3in) square plus seam allowance
- 18 pieces of white fabric, 7.5cm (3in) square plus seam allowance
- 18 small pieces of floral fabric for the hearts, at least 4cm (1½in) square
- Bondaweb (iron-on interfacing)
- Red embroidery cotton
- Coloured embroidery cotton to match the heart fabrics

For the backing

- Two pieces of floral fabric, one 47 x 21cm (18½ x 8¼in) plus seam allowance and one 47 x 31cm (18½ x 12¼in) plus seam allowance
- Cushion pad, 46cm (18in) square
- Three decorative buttons (optional)

Finished size: 46cm (18in) square

Sewing the patchwork

1 Take the 18 pieces of assorted floral fabrics and 18 pieces of white fabric, each measuring 7.5cm (3in) square. Lay out the patchwork squares, alternating between the floral and white fabrics until you are happy with your arrangement.

2 Join up the squares in rows beginning with the first pair, taking care to line the edges up carefully **(a)**. Stitch with a 6mm (¼in) seam allowance using matching embroidery cotton.

TIP If you prefer, you can alternatively use the English paper piecing method (see Hexagon Sewing Set) to construct your patchwork.

a
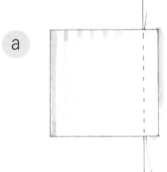

3 Join the rows together, placing a pin between the corners of each square and the next to align the squares correctly (b). Press the patchwork carefully.

b

2 Take the small pieces of floral fabric that you wish to use for the hearts and apply Bondaweb (iron-on interfacing) onto the back of each scrap. Place the heart templates on the back of each fabric scrap and draw around with a pencil.

3 Cut out a heart shape and place on one of the white fabric squares. Iron in place and sew around with blanket stitch using matching embroidery cotton. Repeat for each appliqué heart.

4 Finish off the decoration by stitching a row of running stitch around each heart using two strands of red embroidery cotton. Press the patchwork carefully.

Sewing the appliqué

1 Copy a variety of heart shapes (see Templates) onto card. You will need 18 hearts of varying shapes and sizes.

Making up the cushion

1 Take the piece of backing fabric measuring 47 x 31cm (18½ x 12½in) plus seam allowance, fold one long side in by 6mm (¼in) and hem. Press and place over the smaller piece of backing fabric, aligning the edges carefully. Pin in place (c).

c

Hearts and Flowers Cushion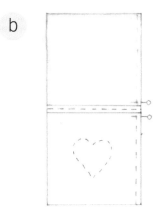

2 Place the backing fabric pieces and the patchwork front piece right sides together and pin in place (d). Sew around all four sides of the cushion.

3 Trim the seams and clip the corners to reduce thickness. Remove the pins holding the two back pieces in place along the centre back.

4 Turn the cushion right way out and press the seams. Fold the centre back pieces neatly and add three buttons for decoration along the fold line. Insert a 46cm (18in) square cushion pad into the opening on the back of the cushion.

d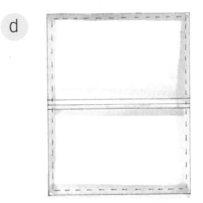

TIP For a pretty finishing touch, add some interesting buttons to the back of your cushion.

  Hearts and Flowers Cushion

Templates

APPLIQUÉ HEARTS
Hearts x 8

Little House Log Cabin Pillow

This homely design featuring a pretty polka dot house surrounded by flowers is created using log cabin effect patchwork and appliqué techniques. The patchwork method is surprisingly simple to achieve and by using different coloured strips of floral fabric, the pillow is given a contemporary twist that suitably frames the charming house design within it. This delightful pillow would make the perfect housewarming gift for a friend, or why not keep it for yourself and use it to brighten up a corner of your own home?

You will need

- White fabric (for patchwork foundation), 28 x 26.5cm (11 x 10¾in)
- White fabric, 10cm (4in) square
- Floral stripe backing fabric, 28 x 26.5cm (11 x 10¾in)
- Two strips of green floral fabric, 5 x 13cm (2 x 5in) and 5 x 8.5cm (2 x 3¼in) plus seam allowance
- Two strips of blue floral fabric, 5 x 13cm (2 x 5in) and 5 x 18cm (2 x 7in) plus seam allowance
- Two strips of yellow floral fabric, 5 x 21.5cm (2 x 8½in) and 5 x 17cm (2 x 6¾in) plus seam allowance
- Two strips of pink floral fabric, 5 x 22cm (2 x 8½in) and 5 x 26cm (2 x 10½in) plus seam allowance
- Scraps of dotty and stripy fabric for the appliqué
- Embroidery cotton to match the appliqué fabrics
- Bondaweb (iron-on interfacing)
- One yellow spotty button
- Cushion pad, 27 x 25.5cm (10½ x 10in)

Finished size: 27 x 25.5cm (10½ x 10in)

Sewing the appliqué house

1 Take the 10cm (4in) square of white fabric and carefully press with an iron.

2 Apply Bondaweb (iron-on interfacing) to the back of the dotty and stripy fabrics that you wish to use for your appliqué house.

3 Trace the templates for the house, roof and chimney (see Templates) and transfer them onto thin card. Cut out the card and use these shapes to draw around to make your house.

4 Use the templates to cut out a small rectangle of plain turquoise fabric for the window and a small rectangle of stripy fabric for the door. Cut out the roof and chimney shapes from stripy fabric.

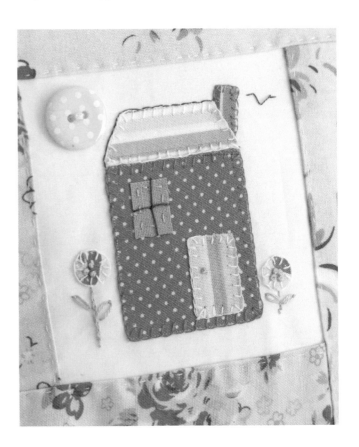

Little House Log Cabin Pillow

5 Arrange the pieces of your house appliqué in the centre of the white fabric square then peel off the paper backing from the Bondaweb and iron the pieces in position one at a time.

6 Sew around the house, roof, chimney and door using blanket stitch and matching embroidery cotton. Sew running stitch around the window and add long stitches in grey embroidery cotton to make the windowpanes. Use grey embroidery cotton to backstitch a line along the roof and add a little bird in the sky.

7 Add two small appliqué circles to form flowers on each side of the house and embroider the stems and leaves using straight stitch and green embroidery cotton.

8 Finally sew on the yellow spotty button in the top left hand corner for the sun.

Making the log cabin cushion

1 Place the appliqué house picture in the centre of the white foundation fabric and pin then tack (baste) in place.

2 Cut two strips of green floral fabric; one measuring 5 x 13cm (2 x 5in) plus seam allowance and one measuring 5 x 8.5cm (2 x 3¼in) plus seam allowance. Lay the shorter strip along the left edge and the longer strip along the bottom edge of the appliqué picture and pin in place (a). Sew the green floral strips to the bottom and left-hand side of the cushion.

a

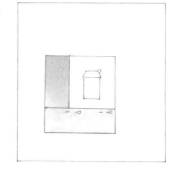

Little House Log Cabin Pillow

3 Cut two strips of blue floral fabric; one measuring 5 x 13cm (2 x 5in) plus seam allowance and another measuring 5 x 18cm (2 x 7in) plus seam allowance. Lay the strips in place as before, with the longer strip along the top edge and the shorter strip along the right edge of the appliqué picture then pin and sew in place (**b**).

b

4 Next cut two strips of yellow floral fabric, one measuring 5 x 21.5cm (2 x 8½in) plus seam allowance and another measuring 5 x 17cm (2 x 6¾in) plus seam allowance. Pin and sew to the bottom and the left-hand sides of the cushion as before.

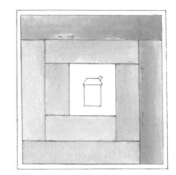

c

5 Finally cut two strips of pink floral fabric, one measuring 5 x 22cm (2 x 8½in) plus seam allowance and another measuring 5 x 26cm (2 x 10½in) plus seam allowance. Pin and sew to the top and right-hand sides of the cushion (**c**).

TIP

If you make non-standard size cushion covers like this one, you can make a simple cushion pad to fit. Cut two pieces of white fabric measuring the same size as the finished cushion plus seam allowance. Sew around all the sides, leaving a small gap for turning. Trim the seams and clip the corners, turn out to the right side and press. Fill the cushion pad with polyester stuffing and sew the gap closed.

Little House Log Cabin Pillow

6 Take the backing fabric and with right sides together, sew around the cushion, leaving a gap for turning (you can insert a zip at the bottom of the cushion if you wish). Trim the seams and clip the corners then turn the right way out and press. Insert the cushion pad and close the gap.

Templates

APPLIQUÉ HOUSE

House

Roof

Window

Chimney

Door

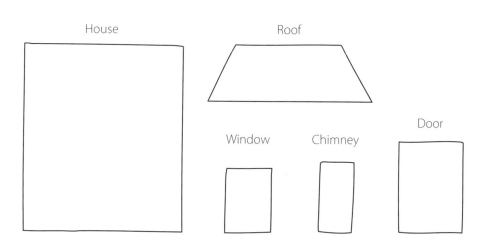

Stuffed Houses

These sweet little houses are so easy to make and such fun to embellish with interesting trims and buttons. There are three different sizes shown here, but they are all made using the same simple method. I have listed the fabric colours for the larger house in the You Will Need list, but feel free to experiment with your own colour combinations for the other sizes – they are a great way of using up any scraps of fabric you might have in your stash. You won't want to stop at one and will soon be sewing the whole street!

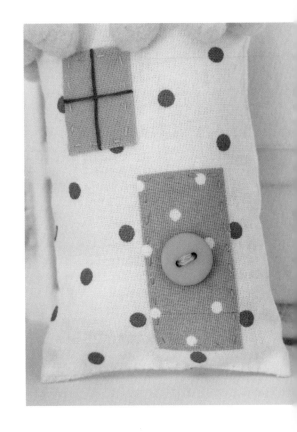

You will need

For the large stuffed house

- Pink and white stripy fabric,
  two pieces 11cm (4¼in) square
- Pink spotty fabric, two pieces 17 x 11cm
  (6¾ x 4¼in) plus seam allowance
- Blue floral fabric for door,
  8.5 x 4.5cm (3¼ x 1¾in)
- Purple spotty fabric for window,
  4cm (1½in) square
- Yellow floral fabric for yo-yo,
  8cm (3¼in) square
- Turquoise bobble trim,
  12cm (4½in) (optional)
- Bondaweb (iron-on interfacing)
- Polyester toy filling
- Embroidery cotton to match
  door and window
- Sewing cotton to match house fabric
- Thin white card
- One yellow button

Finished sizes:

For the rectangular part of the house:

Large house: 17 x 11cm (6¾ x 4¼in)

Medium house: 12.5 x 10cm (5 x 4in)

Small house: 10 x 6.5cm (4 x 2½in)

Roof shape is supplied as a separate

template for each house (see Templates)

Making the large stuffed house

1 Cut two pieces of pink spotty fabric measuring 17 x 11cm (6¾ x 4¼in) plus seam allowance. Cut two pieces of pink and white stripy fabric for the roof measuring 11cm (4¼in) square.

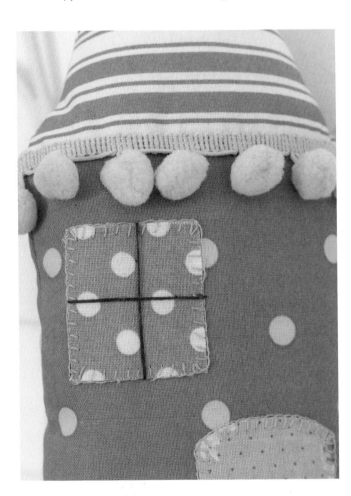

2 Apply Bondaweb (iron-on interfacing) onto the back of the purple spotty and blue floral fabric.

3 Trace the window and door templates (see Templates) onto thin white card and cut out. Use the templates to cut out the window from the purple spotty fabric and the door from the blue floral fabric. Cut out and place them on the house front fabric. Iron on then blanket stitch around using matching embroidery cotton. Add the windowpanes in backstitch using black embroidery cotton.

4 Take the front and back pieces of the pink spotty fabric for the house and with right sides together, sew these to the pink and white stripy fabric pieces for the roof. Press carefully (a).

5 Trace the roof (see Templates) onto the thin white card and cut out carefully. With right sides together, draw around the roof on one side of the pink and white stripy fabric.

6 Sew around the sides and roof of the house, leaving a gap at the bottom for turning (b).

7 Turn the house the right way out and press. Stuff the house firmly with the polyester toy filling and sew the gap closed. **Repeat for the medium and small houses, using smaller amounts of fabric and the templates provided (see Templates).**

Adding embellishments

1 Sew on any extra buttons or trims that you choose. For the large house, I added a turquoise bobble trim around the top and bottom of the roof and a yellow button for the door handle.

2 To make a yo-yo embellishment, start with a circle of fabric measuring twice the size that you want the finished yo-yo to be – here I used a piece of yellow floral fabric measuring 8cm (3¼in) square. Fold the edge over all around by 6mm (¼in) and sew around using running stitch with a strong thread **(c)**.

3 Pull the thread up to gather the fabric into the centre so that only a small gap remains **(d)**. Secure the thread and press the yo-yo then attach with a few slipstitches or a spot of fabric glue. You can add buttons or beads to the centre if you wish.

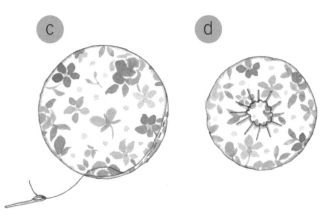

Templates

SMALL HOUSE

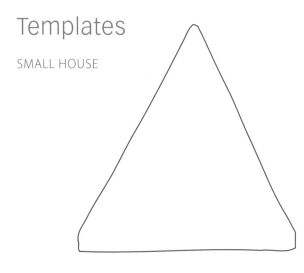

Roof

Door

Window

Stuffed Houses

MEDIUM HOUSE

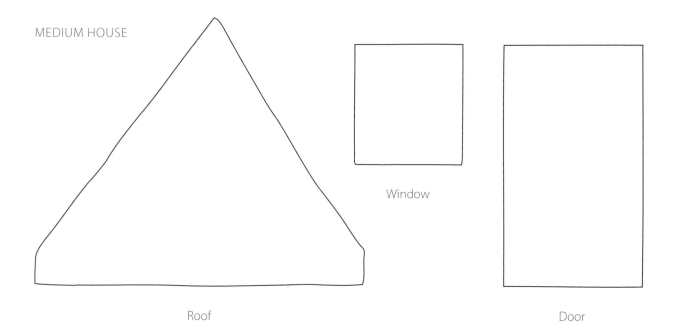

Roof

Window

Door

LARGE HOUSE

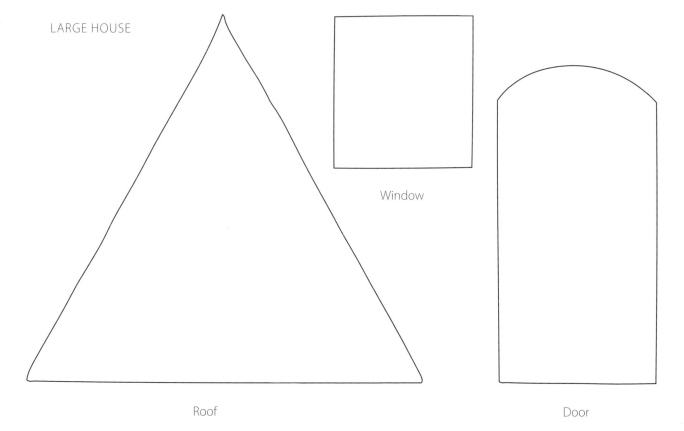

Roof

Window

Door

Romantic French Heart

This pretty stitched heart uses several floral, creamy fabrics and a little embroidery to create a soft and delicate decoration, perfect for a romantic boudoir. I love using fabric prints that have a vintage postcard look, especially when they feature flowers in the design. Adding yo-yo embellishments, charms, buttons and beads gives an interesting three-dimensional look and allows you to really put your own stamp on the project. For a delightful finishing touch, fill the heart with dried scented flowers or rose petal pot pourri, or dot it with a floral essential oil to make it smell as good as it looks!

You will need

- Novelty postcard printed fabric, 50 x 56cm (20 x 22in) plus seam allowance
- Backing fabric, 22 x 13.5cm (8½ x 5¼in)
- Scrap of pink and white spotted printed fabric
- Scrap of pink, green and cream floral fabric
- Scraps of pink fabric for making yo-yos
- Strip of cream cotton lace
- Polyester toy filling
- Pink embroidery cotton
- Six pearl beads
- Two tiny vintage key charms
- One vintage pearly button
- Pale pink satin ribbon to hang, 30cm (12in)

Finished size: 22 x 13.5cm (8½ x 5¼in)

Sewing the heart

1 For the front of the heart, sew together three pieces of printed fabrics to make a patchwork piece measuring 22 x 13.5cm (8½ x 5¼in) plus seam allowance **(a)**. Press the patchwork carefully.

2 Using two strands of pink embroidery cotton, sew a row of cross stitch over the vertical seam. Slipstitch the strip of cream cotton lace along the horizontal seam **(b)**.

3 Take the piece of backing fabric and place right sides together.

4 Trace the heart shape (see Template) onto a piece of thin card to make a template and cut out carefully. Draw around the template onto the patchwork and backing fabrics.

 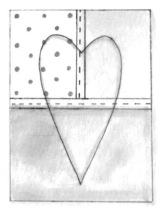

 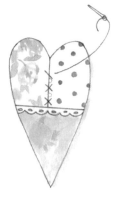

Romantic French Heart

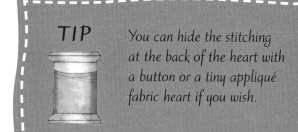

TIP

You can hide the stitching at the back of the heart with a button or a tiny appliqué fabric heart if you wish.

7   Create yo-yo embellishments from scraps of pink fabric (see Steps 2 and 3 of Sewing on embellishments, Stuffed Houses). Sew on the key charms, yo-yos and clusters of large pearl beads.

8   Sew the satin ribbon to the top of the heart in a loop for hanging and add a vintage pearly button.

Template

Template shown at 50% size, enlarge by 200%

HEART

5   Sew around the heart shape then carefully cut a small slit in the centre back piece **(c)**. Turn out the heart, making sure you press out all of the details.

6   Stuff the heart with polyester toy filling, adding any pot pourri or dried scented flowers as desired, and sew up the gap at the back.

c

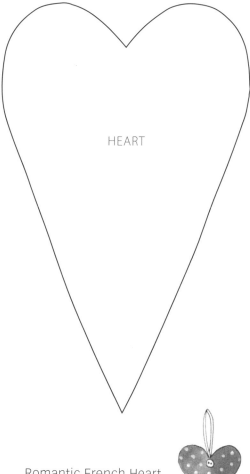

Romantic French Heart   27

Patchwork Boxes

Decorating boxes with a patchwork of ribbon or fabric strips is so easy and fun to do. You can make each one truly unique by using any size of box, painting it in any shade then embellishing it as you choose, providing the perfect opportunity be creative and raid your fabric stash! I used papier-mâché boxes and painted them first then decorated them with an array of coloured and patterned ribbons, strips of selvedge and stickers. Decorated boxes are perfect for presenting a small gift in a really special way; the little turquoise box is an ideal size to contain the Floral Brooch project.

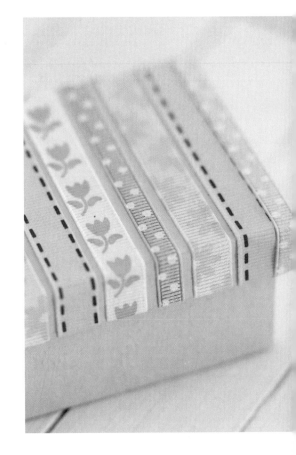

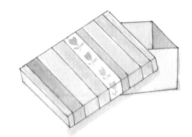

You will need

- Small lidded boxes (see sizes below)
- Emulsion paint in your chosen shade
- Coloured paper to cover the box lids
- Assorted adhesive ribbons
- Assorted strips of selvedge
- Double-sided tape
- Small paintbrush
- Floral stickers (optional)

Finished sizes:

Large box: 9.5 x 7 x 4cm (3¾ x 2¾ x 1½in)

Medium box: 9 x 6.5 x 4cm (3½ x 2½ x 1½in)

Small box: 6.5 x 6.5 x 4cm (2½ x 2½ x 1½in)

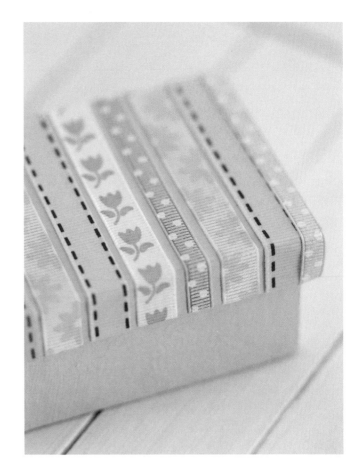

Making the blue ribbon patchwork box

1 Paint the box with pale blue emulsion paint, both inside and outside. Allow it to dry then apply a second coat of paint.

2 When the paint is completely dry, cut strips of adhesive ribbons in your chosen colours and styles. Apply in even stripes across the top of the box lid, pressing them neatly inside.

3 Glue a piece of coloured, patterned paper inside the lid to hide the ribbon ends.

Patchwork Boxes

Making the pink and red selvedge boxes

1 Paint the boxes with emulsion paint in your chosen colours. When the paint is dry, take your pieces of selvedge, cut the correct length to go across the box lid and tuck inside.

2 Attach strips of double-sided tape to the selvedge strips, then peel them off and attach to the box lid, overlapping each one slightly with the next. Glue pieces of coloured paper inside the lids.

3 Add floral stickers to decorate the sides of the boxes if you wish.

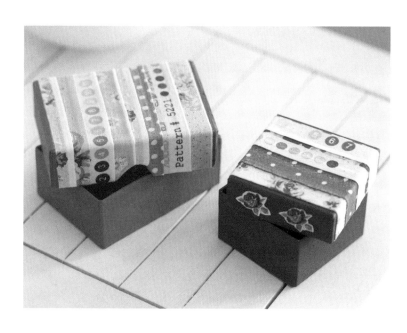

TIP
You could also glue buttons or beads to the boxes for extra embellishment.

Floral Brooch

This simple little fabric brooch is handy for putting pretty little fabric scraps to good use. Quick to create with a little appliqué and embroidery, it makes a sweet little gift to brighten up somebody's day and is perfect for beginners who don't want to tackle a larger project. I love the striking contrast between the bold colours of the simple floral motif and the delicate pastel background fabric. You could present it in a hand-decorated box (see Patchwork Boxes) to really delight the recipient.

You will need

- Scraps of blue, cream and pink floral fabric
- Scraps of red and green spotty fabric
- Embroidery cotton in red and green
- Bondaweb (iron-on interfacing)
- Polyester toy filling
- Small pad of felt, 3 x 1.5cm (1¼ x ⅝in)
- Brooch pin
- Hot glue gun or strong fabric glue
- Thin white card

Finished size: 7 x 5cm (2¾ x 2in)

Making the floral brooch

1 For the front of the brooch, join a piece of cream floral fabric to a piece of blue floral fabric so that the finished size is 7 x 5cm (2¾ x 2in) plus seam allowance.

2 Apply a piece of Bondaweb (iron-on interfacing) onto a scrap of red and green spotty fabric, leaving the paper backing on for now.

3 Trace the flower and leaf shapes (see Template) onto a piece of thin white card, repeating one of the leaves, and cut out carefully. Place the flower template onto the red spotty fabric and cut out. Repeat with the three leaves on green spotty fabric.

4 Remove the paper backing from the flower and leaves and tuck two leaves slightly under the flower on the brooch front (a). Carefully iron in place.

5 Sew around the red flower using blanket stitch and red embroidery cotton. Use green embroidery cotton to blanket stitch around two of the leaves.

TIP

You could use the floral motif on a greetings card or to decorate a box or bag.

Floral Brooch

6 Take the third leaf and iron another piece of green spotty fabric onto the back then cut around the edge to make it double-sided. Stitch around the edge of the leaf using blanket stitch then sew it to the brooch front at just one end, so that it lifts slightly (b).

7 Embroider a green leaf in simple running stitch and another in red (c).

b

c

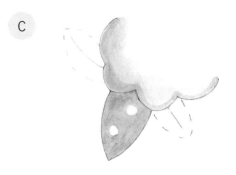

8 Take the pink floral backing fabric and with right sides together, sew around the whole brooch leaving a small gap at the bottom for turning.

9 Turn right side out and press then stuff with polyester toy filling and sew the gap closed. Using red embroidery cotton, sew a row of running stitch around the outside of the whole brooch.

10 Finally glue a small pad of felt to the centre back and using a hot glue gun or strong fabric glue, attach a brooch pin to the felt.

Template

FLOWER AND LEAVES

Floral Brooch

Home Sweet Home Hanger

This pretty little hanger features a cute blue floral birdhouse with a matching pink bird and stuffed flower. It would look charming hung in a garden room or summerhouse, or could be given as a delightful housewarming gift. Make it using leftover scraps of your favourite floral fabrics, or buy a special set of floral fat quarters to mix and match. It is easy to assemble using baker's twine and you can really make it your own by adding a little embellishment to the bottom of the hanger, such as the beautiful decorative egg that I have chosen here.

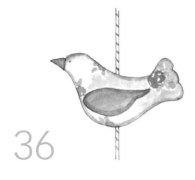

You will need

- Two pieces of blue floral fabric, 8.5 x 13.5cm (3¼ x 5¼in) plus seam allowance
- Scraps of pink floral, pink spotty and red fabric
- Bondaweb (iron-on interfacing)
- Embroidery cotton in black and pale blue
- White sewing cotton
- Red and white baker's twine
- Red and blue buttons
- Polyester toy filling
- Tiny decorative egg (optional)
- Thin card

Finished sizes:

Birdhouse: 15 x 10.5cm (5⅞ x 4⅛in)

Bird: 14 x 8cm (5½ x 3⅛in)

Stuffed flower: 7 x 7cm (2¾ x 2¾in)

Making the birdhouse

1 Place the two blue floral fabric rectangles right sides together and sew around, leaving a gap at the bottom. Turn right side out and press then fill with polyester toy filling. Sew up the gap once filled.

2 Trace the birdhouse roof (see Templates) onto thin card. Draw around the card template on the back of the pink spotty fabric. With right sides together, sew around the shape, leaving one end open for turning. Turn right side out, press and sew up the gap. Running stitch or top stitch along the top edges of the roof with matching embroidery cotton.

3 Place the roof on top of the birdhouse, matching the central point, then slipstitch in place using matching embroidery cotton.

4 Apply Bondaweb (iron-on interfacing) onto a red fabric circle and iron in place below the roof. Sew a red button in the centre of the birdhouse.

Sewing the bird

1 Trace the tummy insert, wing and bird body templates (see Templates) onto thin card. Draw around them onto the back of the pink floral fabric.

2 With right sides together, sew around the bird shape then sew in the gusset for the tummy as marked on the bird body template, leaving a small gap. Turn right side out, fill firmly with polyester toy filling then sew the gap closed.

3 Apply Bondaweb onto pink spotty fabric and trace on the wing shapes. Cut them out and iron one to each side of the bird's body.

4 Make a beak from red embroidery cotton and sew on to the front of the bird's head. Sew two French knots for the eyes with black embroidery cotton.

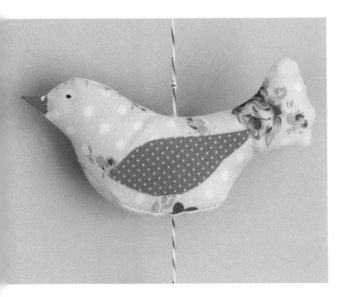

Making the stuffed flower

1 Take two 10cm (4in) squares of pink spotty fabric and place right sides together. Transfer the circle (see Templates) onto one piece. Do not cut out until the sewing is complete.

2 Using matching embroidery cotton, sew around the circle leaving a small gap for turning. Turn the circle out to the right side, stuff with polyester toy filling and sew the gap closed.

3 To form the flower shape use a sharp needle and two strands of blue embroidery cotton. Make eight long threads across the circle, beginning at and returning to the centre each time. Fasten off at the back and add a blue button to the centre front.

Making up the hanger

1 Take the length of red and white baker's twine and thread the needle, then draw it first through the stuffed flower from the base and out through the top. Tie a knot above and below the flower and leave a 10cm (4in) length of twine below the flower.

2 Add the bird and the birdhouse in the same way, tying a knot above and below each one, then draw the twine out through the top of the birdhouse. Leave a 30cm (12in) length of twine and make a large loop for hanging. Attach a small decorative egg to the bottom of the hanger if you wish.

Templates

Templates shown at 50% size, enlarge by 200%
Add seam allowance to each piece

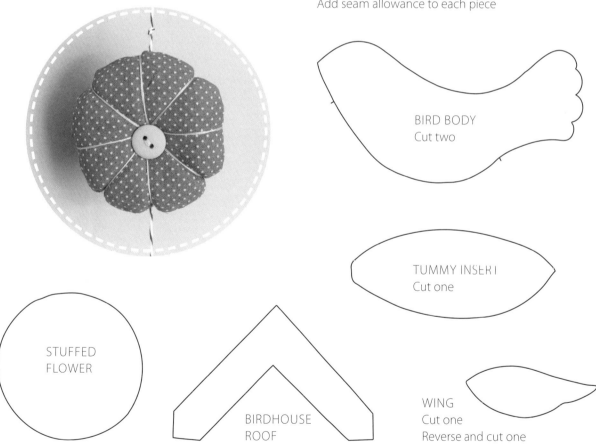

BIRD BODY
Cut two

TUMMY INSERT
Cut one

STUFFED
FLOWER

BIRDHOUSE
ROOF

WING
Cut one
Reverse and cut one

Birdhouse Bunting

It is always fun to hang up some colourful bunting to brighten a corner, prettify a room or add to a celebration. These cute bunting flags are made in the shape of little birdhouses and are very easy to assemble with only a little sewing. You can make the bunting to your chosen length by creating as many or as few birdhouse flags as you wish; they are each made up in the same simple way. They would look especially good in a summerhouse or potting shed, or strung across a garden for a summer party.

You will need

For each flag

- White felt, 11.5 x 7.5cm (4½ x 3in)
- Printed floral fabric,
  11.5 x 8.5cm (4½ x 3¼in)
- Scraps of plain teal and red
  and white spotty fabric
- Bondaweb (iron-on interfacing)
- Pink and white baker's twine
- White sewing cotton
- Hole punch

Finished size:

Each individual birdhouse flag:

10.5 x 7.5cm (4⅛ x 3in)

Sewing the birdhouse flags

1 Apply Bondaweb (iron-on interfacing) onto the back of a piece of floral fabric, cut to size. Follow the manufacturer's instructions to iron the floral fabric onto the white felt.

2 Apply Bondaweb on to the plain teal fabric and trace the two roof pieces (see Templates) onto it. Cut out the pieces and lay them on the top of the birdhouse. Peel off the backing and iron them in place.

3 Cut away the excess fabric and felt from above the birdhouse roof using sharp scissors. Trim the edges of the birdhouse slightly so that the roof overlaps each side.

4 Apply Bondaweb onto the red and white spotty fabric and draw a circle. Cut it out and iron it to the front of the birdhouse.

5 Sew around the birdhouse roof and sides using running stitch and white sewing cotton. Use a small hole punch to make a hole in the roof at each side.

TIP *You could make the whole set in red, white and blue, perfect for a beach hut, summer house or seaside home.*

Making up the bunting

1 Repeat steps 1–5 for Sewing the birdhouse flags to make as many flags as you wish.

2 To assemble the bunting, use pink and white baker's twine to thread the flags through the small punched holes on either side of each roof. Tie a knot at each end of the bunting and leave enough twine for tying wherever you wish to hang it.

TIP

You could use the birdhouse flags to make cheerful plant pokes — just glue a plant stick onto the back of a birdhouse using a glue gun and pop into a flower pot.

Templates

ROOF

1

Overlap
2 here

2

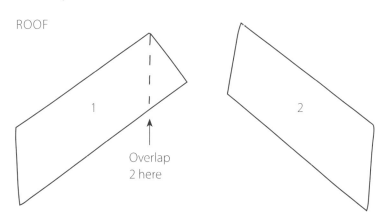

Flower Garland

The stuffed flowers that make up this beautiful garland are so simple to make and the design is so versatile. You can make the garland to any length that you require and the look can be completely transformed by simply varying the colour scheme and decorative buttons used. Here I have selected pretty floral prints that would look lovely hanging up in a garden room, or would brighten up a little girl's bedroom. The stuffed flowers also make delightful pincushions and are a pretty addition to other projects (see Sewing Project Bag).

You will need

For each stuffed flower

- Printed floral fabrics, two 10cm (4in) squares
- Matching sewing cotton
- DMC stranded cotton in contrasting colour
- Polyester toy filling
- Button
- Thin card

For the garland

- Collection of stuffed fabric flowers
- Green and white baker's twine
- Tapestry needle

Finished size:

Each stuffed flower: 10cm (4in) square

Making a stuffed flower

1 Trace the circle (see Template) onto a piece of thin card and cut out carefully.

2 Take two 10cm (4in) squares of floral fabric and place right sides together. On one piece of fabric, draw around the circle template. Do not cut out until the sewing is complete.

3 Using matching sewing cotton, sew around the circle leaving a small gap for turning. Turn out to the right side, stuff with polyester toy filling and sew the gap closed.

TIP For an extra special finishing touch, the stuffed flowers can be scented with lavender or dried rose petals.

4 To form the flower shape, use a sharp needle and two strands of stranded cotton in a contrasting colour. Make eight long threads across the circle, beginning at and returning to the centre each time (a). Fasten off at the back of the flower and sew a button onto the centre front.

a

Making the garland

1 Repeat steps 1–4 for Making a stuffed flower to make as many flowers as you wish.

2 To assemble the garland, take the tapestry needle and thread the baker's twine then draw it through the first flower from right to left. Continue in the same way with each flower until they are all added.

3 Tie a knot at each end of the garland. Leave enough twine for tying wherever you wish to hang it.

TIP *The flowers are extremely versatile and can also be used as pincushions, vertical hanging decorations, or as individual flowers to hang from door or drawer knobs.*

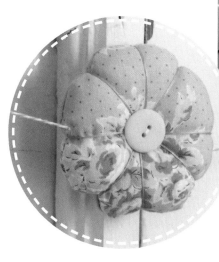

Template

FLOWER

Sugar Bunnies

Making bunnies is something that I love to do. There is something very cute and cuddly about a bunny that appeals to anyone of any age. This adorable trio are each made in the same way and I have named them Pansy (yellow), Petunia (pink) and Bluebell. I used a variety of pretty floral fabrics for their dresses and ears, while making the bunnies themselves in subtle pastel shades of linen to make them reminiscent of sugared almonds. Have fun adapting the basic bunny pattern to any colour you wish, perhaps using recycled linen clothing or vintage fabrics for a cute, retro feel.

You will need

For the bunnies

- Pastel linen, 50 x 70cm (20 x 28in)
- Scraps of matching printed floral fabric
- DMC stranded cotton in brown, black and deep pink
- Polyester toy filling
- Thin card
- Lipstick, fabric paint or blusher (optional)

For each dress

- Floral fabric, 56 x 50cm (22⅜ x 20in)
- Matching sewing cotton
- Two tiny buttons

Finished size:

Each bunny: 33cm (13in) in height

Sewing the bunnies

1 Trace the bunny body, arm and leg shapes (see Templates) onto thin card and cut out carefully. Fold the pastel linen in half and trace the card templates onto it. Do not cut out until the sewing is complete. Sew around the body, arms and legs.

2 Trace the ear shape (see Templates) onto thin card and cut out two ears from the pastel linen. Trace the ear template on to the matching floral fabric and cut out two linings. Place right sides together and sew around the ear, leaving a gap at the bottom. Cut out all of the shapes then turn right side out and press.

3 Stuff the body with polyester toy filling and sew up along the bottom with the seam facing front middle. Stuff the legs and sew on to the bottom of the body with the feet facing forwards. Stuff the arms and sew to either side of the body (a).

4 Sew a line of running stitch along each ear opening then make a small tuck in the base of the each ear to gather (b). Sew to either side of the head.

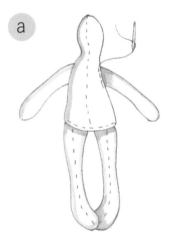

a

b

Sugar Bunnies

5 Sew a nose in satin stitch using deep pink stranded cotton, a mouth in backstitch using brown stranded cotton and two French knots for eyes using black stranded cotton. Sew long stitches on the paws in brown stranded cotton, as shown.

Sewing the dresses

1 Pansy and Bluebell's dresses are the same size; Petunia's dress is simply a longer sleeved version of the pattern, with a longer length skirt too.

2 Trace the pattern for the bodice front and back (see Templates) onto floral fabric, adding a seam allowance. Next trace two sleeves, placing the top of the sleeve against the fold line.

3 For the skirt, cut a piece of floral fabric measuring 26 x 11cm (10½ x 4¼in) plus seam and hem allowances.

TIP For a rosy complexion, add a little circle of lipstick, fabric paint or blusher to the bunny's cheeks.

4 Join the bodice front to the back pieces at the shoulders. Mark the centre of the sleeves and match to the centre of the shoulders, then sew in the sleeves (c). Sew up the bodice side seams and the lower sleeve seams.

5 Hem the skirt, fold the top down by 6mm (¼in) and sew along. Make tucks along the top edge, pinning in place until it matches the width of the bodice, then tack (baste) and sew to the bodice (d). Sew up the back seam of the skirt.

6 Turn in the neck and sew a row of running stitch around it using matching sewing cotton.

7 Turn in the back of the bodice and sew a row of running stitch along it using matching sewing cotton. Add two tiny buttons at the back of the dress, as shown.

c

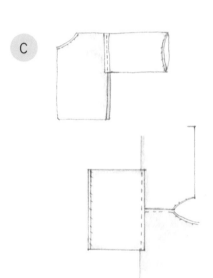

d

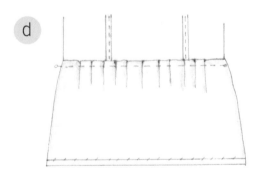

TIP

To decorate the dresses, you could also use patches sewn on with big stitches, a fabric yo-yo with a button centre, a bright bow, or some extra little buttons here and there.

Sugar Bunnies

Templates

Templates shown at 50% size, enlarge by 200%
Add seam allowance to each template

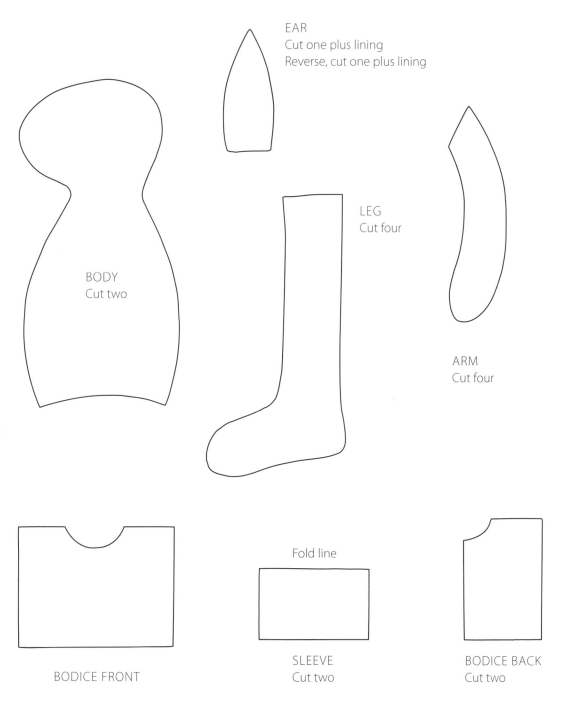

EAR
Cut one plus lining
Reverse, cut one plus lining

LEG
Cut four

ARM
Cut four

BODY
Cut two

Fold line

BODICE FRONT

SLEEVE
Cut two

BODICE BACK
Cut two

Little Hexagon Quilt

This gorgeous little doll's quilt is made using the English paper piecing technique, which involves copying hexagonal templates onto pieces of scrap paper and tacking fabric around them to make little fabric hexagons for patchworking. It is a simple, fun method that gives impressive results. Here, I made my little hexagons from assorted scraps of floral, striped and polka dot fabrics in an array of colours to give maximum visual interest. The red bias binding and matching spotty buttons add a striking finishing touch and the quilt can be flipped over to reveal a bright and bold backing fabric which is sure to delight!

You will need

- Plain white fabric, 40 x 36cm (16 x 14¼in)
- Colourful backing fabric,
  40 x 36cm (16 x 14¼in)
- Wadding (batting), 40 x 36cm (16 x 14¼in)
- Scraps of assorted colourful printed fabrics
- Curved quilting pins
- Red and white spotty bias binding
- White sewing cotton
- Red embroidery cotton
- Four red spotty buttons
- Thin card
- Scrap paper
- Sharp pencil

Finished size: 37.5 x 33cm (14¾ x 13in)

Sewing the patchwork

1 Trace the hexagon (see Template) onto thin card. Place the card template onto a piece of scrap paper and draw around it carefully with a sharp pencil. Repeat 59 times on the same sheet of paper and carefully cut out the hexagons.

2 Cut out the fabric pieces, leaving a 6mm (¼in) seam allowance all the way around. Fold the fabric neatly around the paper hexagons and tack (baste) in place.

3 Join the hexagons by placing them right sides together and oversewing the seams with small stitches. Keep joining the hexagons until the arrangement matches the diagram **(a)**. Remove the papers and press the patchwork, keeping the hems on the outer edges turned under.

4 Place the patchwork in the centre of the white fabric, pin in position then slipstitch in place around the outer edges of the patchwork.

a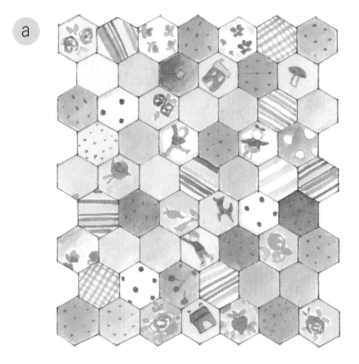

Making the quilt

1 Take the backing fabric and the wadding (batting) and make a quilt sandwich with the patchwork on the top, the backing fabric on the bottom and the wadding in the middle. Pin the layers together with curved quilting pins to hold them securely in place.

2 Using white cotton, quilt around each hexagon (b), smoothing the layers and moving the quilting pins as you go. When all the hexagons are quilted, use two strands of red embroidery cotton to sew a decorative running stitch around the outside of the hexagon patchwork, as shown above.

3 To finish the white border, stitch a line of simple white quilting stitch from the point of each hexagon to the outer edge of the quilt (c).

4 Bind the quilt with red and white spotty bias binding. Sew a red spotty button onto each corner for decoration.

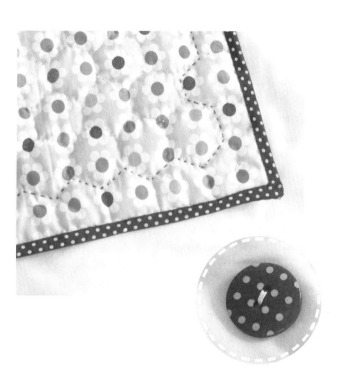

TIP You could use this small hexagon template for all kinds of other projects like making colourful pincushions, mug mats or table mats.

Template

HEXAGON

Daisy's House Quilt

This lovely doll's quilt would make a delightful present for any little girl. The pretty house and garden scene, featuring charming flower, butterfly and heart motifs, is created using simple appliqué techniques and a little embroidery. The floral fabrics were chosen for their complementary pastel shades that enhance the beauty of the scene and the border strips give the impression that the picture has been framed. The quilted circle and wavy line details give the project texture and dimension for the perfect finishing touch.

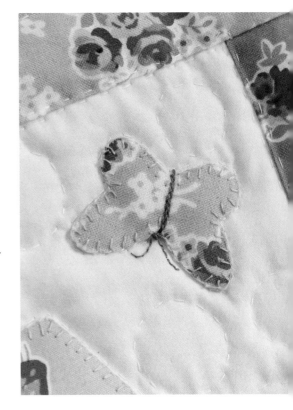

You will need

- Plain white fabric for appliqué backing, 27 x 23cm (10¾ x 9in) plus seam allowance
- Two dark blue floral fabric strips, 32 x 5cm (12¾ x 2in) plus seam allowance
- Two light blue floral fabric strips, 32 x 5cm (12¾ x 2in) plus seam allowance
- Blue patterned backing fabric, 38 x 34.5cm (15 x 13¾in) plus seam allowance
- Wadding (batting), 38 x 34.5cm (15 x 13¾in)
- A selection of fabric pieces for picture in blue floral, blue spotty, pink floral, green spotty, plain green and cream
- Cream floral fabric for bias binding
- Embroidery cotton in blue, dark blue, pink, green and white
- Bondaweb (iron-on interfacing)
- Fine soluble pen

Finished size: 38 x 34.5cm (15 x 13¾in)

Sewing the appliqué picture

1 Trace the appliqué shapes (see Templates) onto thin card and cut them out.

2 Apply Bondaweb (iron-on interfacing) onto the back of the patterned fabric pieces. Cut out a rectangle for the grass from green spotty fabric, measuring 2 x 19cm (¾ x 7½in). Position on the front of the white fabric as shown, peel off the backing and iron in place. Sew around the grass shape using running stitch and white embroidery cotton.

3 Cut out a rectangle from blue spotty fabric for the house, measuring 12 x 8.5cm (4¾ x 3⅜in) and iron on to the picture, as in Step 2. Sew around the house shape using blanket stitch and matching embroidery cotton.

4 Trace the roof and chimney shapes onto blue floral fabric, cut them out and iron in place onto the picture, as in Step 2. The roof should overlap the top of the house slightly. Sew around using blanket stitch and matching embroidery cotton.

5 Carefully cut out a 3.5 x 2.5cm (1⅜ x 1in) window from cream fabric and a 5 x 3.5cm (2 x 1⅜in) door and a 2.5 x 2.5cm (1 x 1in) heart from pink floral fabric. Iron in place, as in Step 2, and sew around using running stitch and white embroidery cotton. Cut out a small circle from white fabric for the door handle. Sew windowpanes using blue embroidery cotton and long stitch.

6 To make the flowers cut out six large circles in pink floral fabric and six smaller circles in white fabric. Apply Bondaweb and attach each flower in place (see Step 2). Sew around the flowers using blanket stitch and pink embroidery cotton then sew around the centres using running stitch and white embroidery cotton. Cut out four leaf shapes from plain green fabric, iron them in place and sew around using running stitch and white embroidery cotton. Sew the stems with green embroidery cotton, couching down a long stitch from the base of the flowers to the base of the leaves.

7 Finally cut out and attach two butterflies from blue floral fabric (see Step 2) and sew around each one using blanket stitch and matching blue embroidery cotton. Sew the antennae and body onto each butterfly using backstitch and dark blue embroidery cotton.

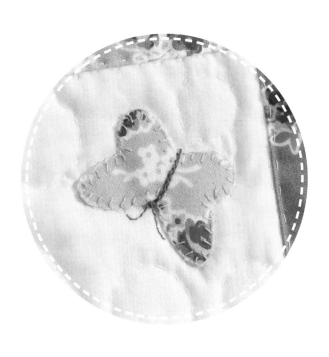

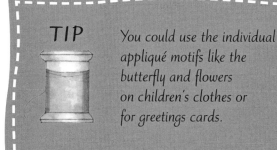

TIP You could use the individual appliqué motifs like the butterfly and flowers on children's clothes or for greetings cards.

Making the quilt

1   Press the picture then position the light and dark blue floral fabric border strips as shown in the photograph, with the dark blue strips at the bottom and right-hand side and the light blue strips at the top and left-hand side. Overlap the strips and sew in place.

2   Using a fine soluble pen, draw small circles for quilting on the white background fabric and a wavy line with a central heart below the grass strip.

3   Take the backing fabric and wadding (batting) and make a quilt sandwich, with the appliqué picture on the top, the blue patterned backing fabric on the bottom and the wadding in the middle. Pin the layers together with curved quilting pins to hold them securely in place while you quilt.

4   Using white embroidery cotton, quilt around the house, the flowers, the butterflies and the circles and wavy line that you have drawn on as a guide.

5   Quilt along the border strips with white embroidery cotton. When all the quilting is complete, use a cloth and cold water to dampen and remove the quilting lines that were drawn on.

Daisy's House Quilt

6 Finally make the bias binding using cream floral fabric. Sew it in place around the quilt and slipstitch down at the back.

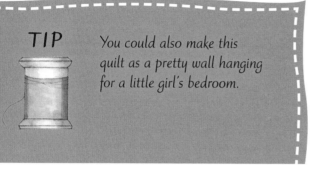

TIP

You could also make this quilt as a pretty wall hanging for a little girl's bedroom.

Templates

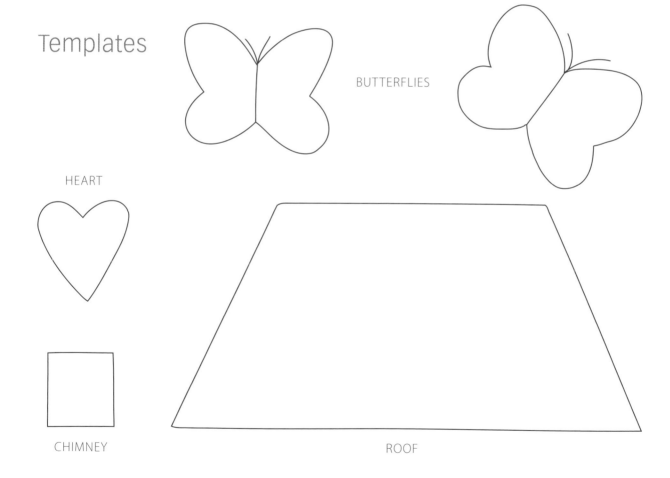

BUTTERFLIES

HEART

CHIMNEY

ROOF

Patchwork Play Cubes

Soft cubes have long been made for little hands to play with and they are still well loved today. Perfect for squeezing, grabbing, throwing and even teething on, babies are fascinated by their shape and texture. This set of three play cubes is made from bright colourful fabrics, with cute appliqué heart and bunny motifs and little ribbon tags that will really appeal to babies. The three sizes will enable little ones to build towers and knock them down again and again!

You will need

For the big bunny cube

- Six fabrics in assorted colours, 11cm (4¼in) square plus seam allowance
- White fabric, 11cm (4¼in) square
- Scraps of pink floral, red and white striped and red and white check fabric
- Pink and blue gingham ribbon
- Deep pink stitch edge ribbon

For the sweetheart cube

- Six pieces of pink and cream patterned fabric, 8.5cm (3¼in) square plus seam allowance
- White fabric, 6cm (2⅜in) square
- Three pink and white ribbon scraps

For the tiny bunny cube

- Six pieces of coloured printed fabric, 6cm (2⅜in) square plus seam allowance
- White fabric, 5cm (2in) square
- Four assorted scraps of colourful ribbons

For each patchwork cube

- Embroidery cotton in white, black and blue
- Matching sewing cotton
- Polyester toy filling
- Bondaweb (iron-on interfacing)

Finished sizes:

Big bunny cube: 11cm (4¼in) cubed

Sweetheart cube: 8.5cm (3¼in) cubed

Tiny bunny cube: 6cm (2⅜in) cubed

Sewing the big bunny cube

1 Apply the Bondaweb (iron-on interfacing) onto the white fabric, a scrap of pink floral fabric and a scrap of red and white check fabric.

2 Trace the big bunny appliqué shape (see Templates) onto the back of the white fabric and draw circles measuring 3cm (1¼in) in diameter onto the back of the red and white check and striped fabric. Cut out the appliqué shapes and a floral motif from the pink floral fabric.

3 Take one of the coloured fabric squares, iron the big bunny shape onto the centre then sew around it using blanket stitch and one strand of white embroidery cotton. Embroider an eye using two strands of black embroidery cotton. Iron on the floral patch and sew around it using blanket stitch and one strand of white embroidery cotton.

4 Take another coloured fabric square and iron on the red and white check appliqué circle in the bottom left-hand corner. Sew around it using running stitch in blue embroidery cotton. Repeat with the red and white striped circle on another of the fabric squares.

5 One-by-one, by hand or machine, sew together the six sides of the cube 6mm (¼in) from the edges. Sew little pieces of folded ribbon into the seams where desired, to form little tags.

6 Leave the last side open for turning and stuffing. Turn out the cube to the right side, pushing all the corners out carefully. Stuff firmly with polyester toy filling and neatly stitch the last side closed.

Sewing the sweetheart cube

Follow Steps 1–6 for the Big Bunny Cube using the 8.5cm (3¼in) pink and cream patterned fabric squares. This time, trace and cut out the heart shape (see Templates) from the white fabric and sew around it onto one of your coloured fabric squares using blanket stitch and white embroidery cotton.

Sewing the tiny bunny cube

Follow Steps 1–6 for the Big Bunny Cube using the 6cm (2⅜in) coloured fabric squares. Trace and cut out the tiny bunny shape (see Templates) from white fabric and sew around it onto one of your coloured fabric squares using blanket stitch and white embroidery cotton. Embroider an eye using black embroidery cotton.

Templates

Templates shown at 50% size, enlarge by 200%

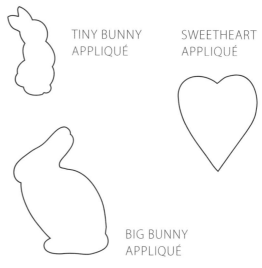

TINY BUNNY APPLIQUÉ

SWEETHEART APPLIQUÉ

BIG BUNNY APPLIQUÉ

Pippi Doll

This friendly doll is perfect for hanging in a child's room and the many little pockets on her dress can be used to store small trinkets or sweets. Pippi was inspired by the wonderful Scandinavian elf dolls, some of which are made as Advent calendars with treats in their numbered pockets. She would make a lovely birthday present for a little girl, who will love the little surprises or sweets tucked into the pockets. You will also find a pattern here for the cute little felt bunny that can be seen peeking out of a pocket in Pippi's dress.

You will need

For the doll

- Cream linen, 25cm (10in) square
- Striped jersey fabric, 25cm (10in) square
- Fair curly doll hair
- Polyester toy filling
- Matching sewing cotton
- Embroidery cotton in blue and red
- Pink fabric paint
- Tiny red bow
- Thin white card

For the doll's dress

- Two pieces of cotton printed fabric, 41.5 x 29.5cm (16¼ x 11½in) plus seam allowance
- Small scraps of patterned fabric for pockets
- Elastic
- Buttons and ribbons to decorate

For the bunny and paper packets

- Two pieces of white felt, 12 x 6cm (4¾ x 2⅜in)
- Embroidery cotton in black, pink, blue and yellow
- White sewing cotton
- Polyester toy filling
- Pink fabric paint
- White card
- Soluble pen
- Old children's book pages, or photocopies
- Narrow ribbons (optional)

Finished size: 57 x 29cm (22¾in x 11⅜in)

Sewing the face and body

1 Trace the pattern for the doll's head and body, arms and legs (see Templates) and transfer them onto thin white card. Carefully cut out around the shapes.

2 Take the piece of cream linen and fold in half. Place the doll's head and body shape on the linen and draw around, without cutting out the shapes.

3 Sew around the head and body shape, leaving a small gap at the bottom for turning and carefully cut out the shapes. Trim the seams and turn right side out. Press then stuff the body with polyester toy filling. Sew the gap closed.

4 For the arms, place a piece of striped jersey fabric right sides together with a piece of linen and sew along a straight seam. Fold the combined piece of fabric right sides together and place the hand and arm pattern template with the hand on the linen and the arm on the striped fabric (a). Draw around then repeat for the second arm, turning the pattern over so that it is mirrored. Sew around both arms and hands, leaving a gap at the bottom then cut out the shapes carefully. Turn to the right side and press then stuff, leaving the tops of the arms fairly loose so that they hang down slightly. Sew along the seam to close.

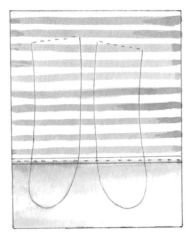

Pippi Doll

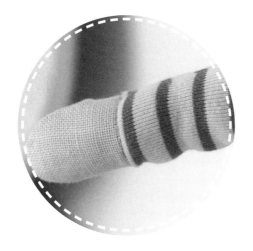

5 Repeat Step 4 using the leg template then sew the arms and legs to the doll's body.

6 Embroider a simple face as shown, using satin stitch and blue embroidery cotton for the eyes , and a line of backstitch in red embroidery cotton for the mouth. Use a little pink fabric paint to make the cheeks look rosy.

7 Place the curly hair around the face and sew in place or use fabric glue to attach. Add a little red bow.

Sewing the dress

1 Trace the patterns for the dress and pockets (see Templates) and transfer them onto thin white card. Carefully cut out around the shapes. Draw around the dress template onto the two pieces of printed fabric, adding seam and hem allowances to the top and bottom and cut out. Draw around the pockets onto seven small scraps of patterned fabric and cut out.

2 Arrange the seven pockets on the front piece of the doll's dress. Fold in the edges of the pockets and sew them to the front of the dress then add any embroidery or button embellishments as desired.

3 Take the front and back fabric pieces and sew up one side seam, leaving a 5cm (2in) gap for the arm, 6.5cm (2½in) down from the top edge.

4 Make a hem along the bottom edge by turning in the top edge by 1.5cm (⅝in) and sewing along. Thread a piece of elastic through the top edge **(b)**.

5 Sew the second side seam, leaving the same size gap for the armhole as in Step 3.

6 Pull up the elastic at the neck to gather it. Place the dress on the doll and when the neckline is pulled up tightly enough, secure the elastic.

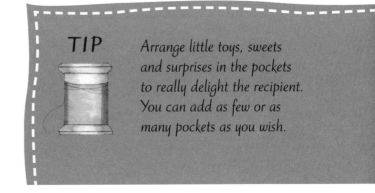

TIP

Arrange little toys, sweets and surprises in the pockets to really delight the recipient. You can add as few or as many pockets as you wish.

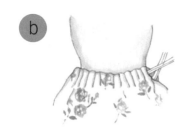

Making the bunny

1 Transfer the felt bunny pattern (see Templates) onto white card and carefully cut out. Take the two pieces of white felt and draw around the bunny template onto one of them using a soluble pen.

2 Use white sewing cotton to sew right around the shape in the two felt layers, leaving a gap at the bottom for stuffing.

3 Carefully cut out all the way around the bunny. Stuff with small amounts of filling then stitch up the bottom neatly.

Pippi Doll

4 Embroider the eyes using French knots and one strand of black embroidery cotton. Use one strand of pink embroidery cotton to embroider a mouth in backstitch and a nose in satin stitch. Use a little pink fabric paint to make the cheeks look rosy.

5 Stitch some small flowers on to the bunny's body, using lazy daisy stitch and one strand of blue embroidery cotton for the petals and French knots and one strand of yellow embroidery cotton for the centres.

Making the paper packets

1 Place a small toy or sweet in the centre of a piece of paper. It is nice to use old children's book pages, or photocopies here for an authentic look.

2 Take a second piece of paper and sew around through the two layers to enclose the gift.

3 When the sewing is finished, tie a small narrow ribbon around the tiny parcel if you wish. When the packet is to be opened, it can be simply torn along the perforated line made by the stitching.

TIP

You could make the doll for a special birthday, adding the number of pockets for the age of the child. Embroider a number on each pocket, or make them from appliqué or using rubber stamps.

Templates

Templates shown at 50% size, enlarge by 200%

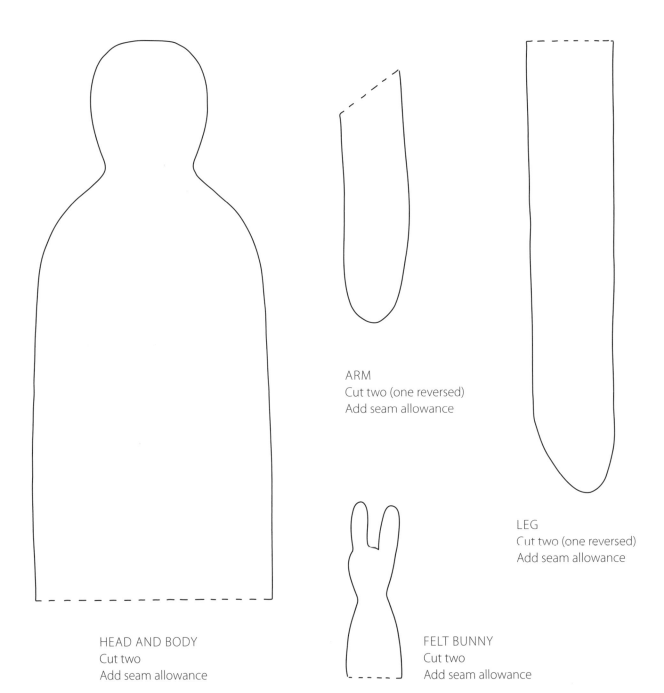

ARM
Cut two (one reversed)
Add seam allowance

LEG
Cut two (one reversed)
Add seam allowance

HEAD AND BODY
Cut two
Add seam allowance

FELT BUNNY
Cut two
Add seam allowance

Pippi Doll

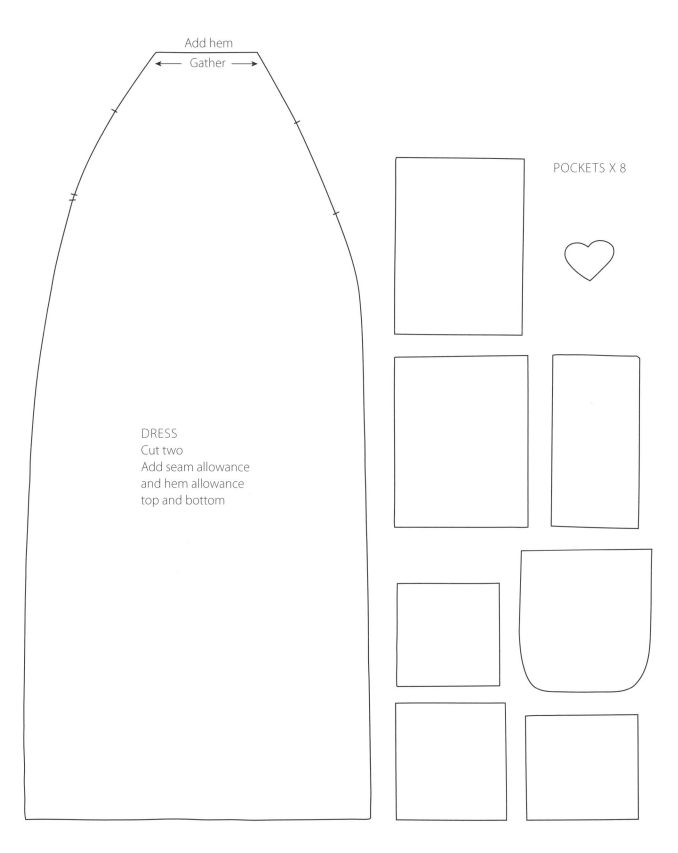

Add hem

← Gather →

POCKETS X 8

DRESS
Cut two
Add seam allowance
and hem allowance
top and bottom

Pippi Doll

Pretty Drawstring Bags

These drawstring bags are quick to make, fun to use and they look just gorgeous too! It is easy to change the colour scheme to suit either a boy or a girl and by adding a simple initial you can give the bag a special personal touch. The drawstring makes the bags easy to open and close even for the smallest hands. Make several to hang in a row in a child's bedroom or they make fantastic bags to hold a school or nursery child's sports kit. Both pretty and practical, they are sure to delight!

You will need

For the pink bag

- Two pieces of pink floral fabric, 36 x 25cm (14¼ x 10in) plus seam allowance and top hem allowance
- White spotty, green polka dot and pink dotty fabric, each piece 10cm (4in) square
- Pink and white striped cord, 80cm (32in) length
- Bondaweb (iron-on interfacing)
- Matching sewing cotton
- Pink embroidery cotton
- Pinking shears

For the blue bag

- Two pieces of blue and white novelty print fabric, 40 x 24cm (16 x 9½in) plus seam allowance and top hem allowance
- Red spotty and blue check fabric, each piece 10cm (4in) square
- Red cord, 70cm (28in) length
- Bondaweb (iron-on interfacing)
- Matching sewing cotton
- Blue embroidery cotton

Finished sizes:

Pink bag: 36 x 25cm (14¼ x 10in)
Blue bag: 40 x 24cm (16 x 9½in)

Making the pink bag

1 Take the two pieces of pink floral fabric and with right sides together, machine sew down one long side with a 6mm (¼in) seam allowance.

2 Turn the top edge down by 3cm (1⅛in) to form the casement and machine sew in place (a).

3 With right sides together, machine sew along the bottom of the bag and down the second long side.

4 Apply Bondaweb (iron-on interfacing) onto the back of the pink dotty fabric. Use a wooden letter template or draw freehand your chosen (reversed) initial onto the back of the pink fabric and cut out carefully.

Pretty Drawstring Bags

Making the blue bag

Follow the instructions for the pink bag, using the two pieces of blue and white novelty print fabric. To sew the patch, take the piece of red spotty fabric, apply Bondaweb onto the back then cut it out so it measures 7.5 x 6cm (3 x 2⅜in). Apply Bondaweb onto the back of the blue check fabric, trace or draw your chosen (reversed) letter onto it and carefully cut it out. Iron the letter to the centre of the red spotty fabric and sew in place using blanket stitch and blue embroidery cotton.

5 Iron the initial onto the green polka dot fabric square and sew around the initial with blanket stitch and pink embroidery cotton. Apply Bondaweb onto the back of the green polka dot square, draw a 7cm (2¾in) diameter circle on the back with the initial in the centre and cut out. Apply Bondaweb onto the back of the white spotty fabric square and cut out an 8.5cm (3¼in) diameter circle using pinking shears.

6 Position the initial patch onto the front of the bag as shown and iron in place. Using two strands of pink embroidery cotton, sew a line of running stitch around the green circle, close to the edge.

7 Thread the pink and white cord through the casement at the top of the bag and pull up, tying the ends in a knot.

TIP

You could write a child's name on a piece of plain fabric and embroider it before sewing on to the bag, or use rubber stamps to print the name or initial onto a circle of fabric before appliquéing.

Lollipop Flowers Picture

Bright fabrics and simple appliqué make this sweet picture a pleasure to create. I love the childlike simplicity of the lollipop-shaped flowers that stand out so beautifully against the pure white background fabric. The picture is a perfect opportunity to use up scraps of your favourite quilt fabrics, as you only need tiny pieces for the flowers and bunting. Add some small decorative buttons and a little embroidery and you will have a special handmade piece to give as a gift or treasure in your own home.

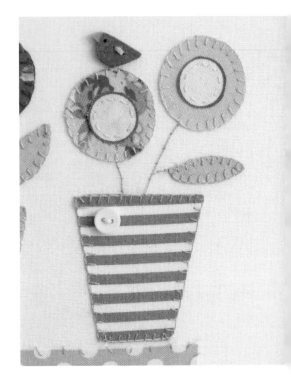

You will need

- White fabric, 36 x 28cm (14¼ x 11in)
- Assorted scraps of floral, striped and spotty fabric
- Bondaweb (iron-on interfacing)
- Embroidery cotton in matching colours, green and purple
- Assorted decorative buttons, Tiny Yellow Bird and Tiny Brown Bird buttons (see Suppliers)
- Thin card

Finished size: 36 x 28cm (14¼ x 11in)

Sewing the picture

1 Trace or photocopy the flower and flowerpot shapes (see Templates), adhere to thin card and cut out carefully. Choose the floral, striped and spotty fabrics that you wish to use for the bottom border, the flowerpots and the flowers and apply Bondaweb (iron-on interfacing) onto the back of them.

2 Cut out a rectangle measuring 2 x 14.5cm (¾ x 5¾in) from green spotty fabric for the bottom border and apply Bondaweb to the back. Peel off the backing and place onto the white fabric. When you are happy with its position, iron in place. Stitch a few small, random straight stitches around the edges using one strand of green embroidery cotton.

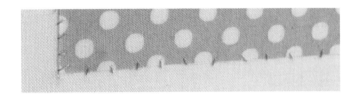

3 Use the templates to cut out three flowerpots from spotty, floral and striped fabric. Position just above the bottom border, iron them in place then blanket stitch around each flowerpot using one strand of matching embroidery cotton.

4 Use the templates to cut out six coloured fabric circles for the flowers and six smaller white fabric circles for the centres. Arrange and iron in place then sew around the outside of each flower using blanket stitch and one strand of matching embroidery cotton. Sew a line of running stitch in white embroidery cotton around the flower centres.

TIP *If you use a large spot fabric for the flowers, you can include a little of the background colour to make an edge.*

5 Cut out three leaf shapes from green fabric, iron in place and sew around each leaf as before. Using one strand of green embroidery cotton, make a long stitch and couch it down to form stems from the base of the flowers to the top of the pots.

6 Apply Bondaweb onto the back of scraps of bright floral fabric and cut out eight tiny triangles for the bunting. Sew a line across the picture using one strand of purple embroidery cotton and couch down, as shown below.

TIP

You can create a tiny decorative quilt with the picture. Using a piece of wadding (batting) and backing fabric, bind with bias binding when finished and simply hang with ribbon.

7 Sew the Tiny Yellow Bird and Tiny Brown Bird buttons (see Suppliers) above the flowers, as shown below. Finally press the work carefully, sew some decorative buttons onto the flowerpots and frame the picture.

Templates

FLOWER AND CENTRE

FLOWERPOT

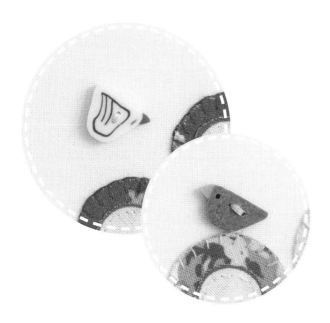

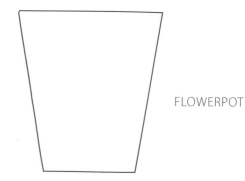

Lollipop Flowers Picture

Patchwork Project Bag

What could be better than a nice, squashy patchwork bag to carry your sewing projects around in? I have designed this padded bag with a few clever little sewing essentials to help you: a tape measure, a stuffed flower that can be used as a pincushion, a pretty little heart pocket for keeping scissors and a large inside pocket for your fabric scraps. It would make a wonderful gift for a crafty friend or can be used to organize your own treasured crafts. Have fun embellishing with ribbons, buttons, yo-yos, mother of pearl – the only limit is your imagination!

You will need

- Floral, check and spotty fabrics, a jelly roll or seven strips measuring 6.5 x 112.5cm (2½ x 44¼in)
- Fusible wadding (batting), 46 x 112cm (18 x 44in)
- Floral lining fabric, 46 x 112cm (18 x 44in)
- Pink polka dot fabric, 46 x 54cm (18 x 21in)
- Red embroidery cotton
- Embellishments: covered button, assorted buttons, tape measure ribbon, etc.

Finished size: 38 x 37cm (15 x 14½in)

TIP

I made this gorgeous bag using a jelly roll of fabric, but you could just cut the strips from fabric in your stash if you prefer.

Sewing the bag

1 Machine sew together seven strips of the jelly roll fabric (or seven strips of fabric measuring 6.5 x 112.5cm (2½ x 44¼in)) and press. Trim the resulting piece of patchwork neatly so that it measures 72cm (28⅜in) long (the leftover piece will be used for a pocket) **(a)**. Fold the patchwork in half. This piece forms the bag front and back.

2 Cut a piece of fusible wadding (batting) to fit the front and back and iron in place.

a

  Patchwork Project Bag

3 Take a strip of jelly roll fabric and iron fusible wadding on to the back. Attach it to the front of the bag at the side seam, making a straight seam along the bottom and sewing up the side seam of the back (b). Repeat the process at the other side.

4 Make a pocket for the inside of the bag by trimming the leftover piece of patchwork to 21 x 16.5cm (8¼ x 6½in) plus seam allowance. Cut a piece the same size to match the bag lining. With right sides together, sew around the pocket, leaving a small gap for turning (c). Turn to the right side and press then sew up the gap.

5 Take the lining fabric and position the pocket on the inside, 12cm (4¾in) down from the top. Sew in place.

6 With right sides together, sew down the left side of the lining, along the bottom and up the right side. Place the lining inside the bag and fold the top edge over the right side of the bag by 4cm (1½in). Topstitch in place using running stitch and red embroidery cotton (d).

7 To make the handles, take one jelly roll fabric strip, fold a 6mm (¼in) edge inwards down both sides and press. Fold the strip of fabric in half and topstitch down the edge. Cut the strip in half and turn in the ends (e). Pin to the front of the bag, 10cm (4in) in from the sides and machine stitch in place. Sew on the back in the same way.

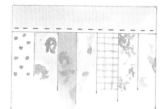

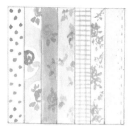

Adding the embellishments

1 To make the heart pocket (for embroidery scissors), take two pieces of pink polka dot fabric measuring 12cm (4¾in) square and with right sides together, draw the heart (see Template) onto the back of one of them. Sew around the whole shape, cut out the heart and make a small slit in the back of it for turning. Turn out and press. Pin the heart onto the front of the bag and sew in place, then topstitch with red embroidery cotton for a decorative finish. Add a pink button.

2 To make a rectangular pocket, take two pieces of pink polka dot fabric measuring 12.5 x 14cm (4¾ x 5½in). With right sides together, sew around the pocket leaving a small gap for turning. Turn to the right side and press then sew in place on the back of the bag.

TIP You could make a matching pretty needle case from the left over scraps, and embellish it with buttons and ribbon.

Patchwork Project Bag

3 Use pink polka dot fabric to make a stuffed flower (see Making a stuffed flower in the Flower Garland chapter) to hang from one of the handles. This will be used as a pincushion.

4 Add a bright pink button in the centre front to loop, add a covered elastic band closure over and decorate your bag as you desire.

Template

HEART
POCKET

TIP To embellish your bag, try adding a piece of twill tape measure ribbon attached with a button, white mother of pearl, decorative buttons and even a yo-yo.

Hexagon Sewing Set

This stylish little set would make the perfect gift for any sewing enthusiast. The pincushion and scissor keeper are made using the English paper piecing method – one of my favourite techniques, which whilst being very accurate, is also a peaceful, relaxing activity. It involves cutting hexagon templates, copying them onto pieces of scrap paper and tacking fabric around them. The hexagons are used in a fun way – the stripes can create different optical effects depending on the direction you place them in. I have used appliqué to decorate this pretty set, which evokes happy thoughts of stripy candy.

You will need

For the pincushion

- Candy-striped pink and white fabric, 50 x 56cm (20 x 22in)
- Scrap of plain white fabric
- Scrap of floral printed fabric
- White sewing cotton
- Polyester toy filling
- Bondaweb (iron-on interfacing)
- Thin cardboard
- Scrap paper
- Sharp pencil

For the scissor keeper

- Scrap of candy-striped pink and white fabric
- Scrap of floral printed fabric
- Polyester toy filling
- Bondaweb (iron-on interfacing)
- Pink cord, 25cm (10in) length
- White sewing cotton
- Two paper hexagons

Finished size:

Pincushion: 16cm (6¼in) width

Scissor keeper: 5.75cm (2¼in) width

Sewing the pincushion

1 Place the hexagon (see Templates) onto a piece of scrap paper and draw around it with a sharp pencil. Repeat 14 times on the same sheet of paper and cut out the hexagons.

2 For the centre front, take a piece of white fabric and cut to fit around a paper hexagon, leaving a 6mm (¼in) seam allowance all the way around. Fold the fabric neatly around the paper hexagon and tack (baste) in place **(a)**. Repeat for the centre back hexagon.

3 Cut 12 pieces of pink and white candy-striped fabric to fit around the paper hexagons. Fold then tack as in Step 2.

4 Take the floral printed fabric and choose a flower motif that will fit in the centre of the white hexagon. Apply Bondaweb (iron-on interfacing) onto the back of the motif and carefully cut out around the shape. Iron the flower motif onto the central white hexagon.

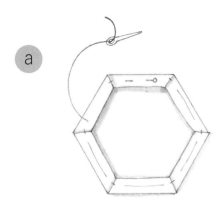

a

Hexagon Sewing Set

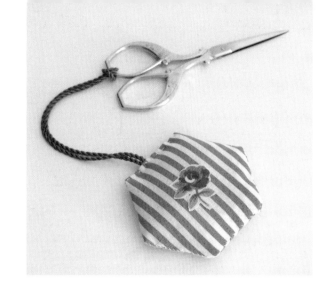

5 Arrange six stripy hexagons around the central appliqué patch. When you are happy with the arrangement, oversew the patches together using white sewing cotton **(b)**.

6 Arrange the pieces for the back in the same way around the central white patch and sew them all together. Press both the front and the back pieces of patchwork then snip the tacking threads and remove the papers (you can re-use them).

7 Place the front and back pieces together and oversew around the edges, leaving the last two edges open for turning **(c)**.

8 Turn the sewn patchwork right side out and push out all the corners neatly. Fill with polyester toy stuffing, making sure it is evenly distributed inside the pincushion. Sew up the last two edges.

Sewing the scissor keeper

1 Cut two pieces of stripy fabric to fit around the paper hexagons, leaving a 6mm (¼in) seam allowance all the way around (see Step 1 for Sewing the pincushion).

2 Iron a small piece of Bondaweb onto the back of the floral printed fabric and cut out a flower motif. Iron this onto the centre of one of the candy-striped fabric hexagons for the front of the scissor keeper.

3 Fold the candy-striped fabric around the paper hexagons carefully and tack in place.

4 With *wrong* sides together, neatly oversew five of the edges, leaving the top edge open **(d)**. Stuff the scissor keeper with polyester toy filling, insert the cord into the open edge then sew it closed.

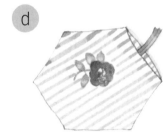

d

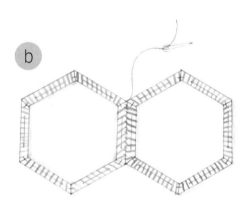

b

c

Template

Template shown at 50% size, enlarge by 200%

HEXAGON

Hexagon Sewing Set

Sewing Heart

This pretty little stuffed heart is the perfect gift for any craft-lover to hang in their home with pride. Simple to create, it is made up from scraps of fabric and decorated with lovely crafty extras such as tags, charms, buttons and rubber stamps – it even hangs from a tape measure ribbon! So fun to make and embellish, you will probably think of lots of ideas as you make this little heart and have a wealth of treasures in your sewing box that you will be eager to add.

You will need

- Pink floral fabric, 16cm (6¼in) square
- Scraps of pink and white floral, plain white and blue spotty fabric
- Piece of selvedge, 7cm (2¾in) length
- Tape measure ribbon, 22cm (8½in) length
- Polyester toy filling
- Bondaweb (iron-on interfacing)
- Matching sewing cotton
- Haberdashery rubber stamps
- Buttons: two pink and one white
- Tiny pink bow
- Scissor charm
- Small gold safety pin
- Thin card

Finished size: 12.5 x 14cm (4¾ x 5½in)

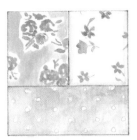

TIP You could also use a novelty fabric with a sewing-themed print to make this heart.

Sewing the heart

1 Trace the heart (see Template) onto thin card and cut out carefully.

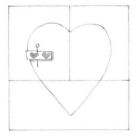

TIP Keep your heart template – you will be able to reuse it and make other hearts very quickly.

2 Piece together three different fabrics: blue spotty, pink floral and white floral, to make a 16cm (6¼in) square for the front of the heart **(a)**. Cut a piece of pink floral fabric the same size for the back.

3 Fold the piece of selvedge in half and press. Pin it to the heart front so that it is caught in the seam when the heart is sewn **(b)**.

a

b

Sewing Heart

4 With right sides together, place the heart template onto the back piece of fabric and draw around it. Do not cut out until the sewing is complete. Sew around the whole heart shape, make a small slit in the centre of the back and turn the heart out to the right side.

5 Press then stuff with polyester toy filling. Sew the gap in the centre back closed.

6 Using haberdashery rubber stamps, stamp two circular designs onto plain white fabric. Apply Bondaweb (iron-on interfacing) onto the back of the fabric then cut the stamped circular designs out. Apply one stamped decoration to the front of the heart and one to the back then iron in place.

7 Sew a white button to the point where the three fabrics join on the front. Add the scissor charm, pink bow, ribbon tag and gold safety pin as shown.

8 Sew on the tape measure ribbon at the centre top of the heart and add a small pink button at the back and the front of the heart.

Template

Template shown at 50% size, enlarge by 200%

SEWING HEART

Stuffed Mushrooms

As a child, I was enchanted by red spotted mushrooms or toadstools in storybooks; especially those that had a little door and window. I can still imagine them having cute little homes inside! A year or so ago I began to make my own stuffed fabric mushrooms to bring a little of that sense of childlike wonder to life. They are simple to create, loved by children and adults alike and look delightful hanging up in a garden room or summerhouse. You could even make a delightful garland by hanging several different sized mushrooms from a spotty ribbon.

You will need

For the large mushroom house

- Red and white spotty fabric, 20cm (8in) square
- White fabric, 20cm (8in) square
- Scraps of blue, green and pink fabric
- Bondaweb (iron-on interfacing)
- Red baker's twine, 20cm (8in) length
- Embroidery cotton in black, blue, green and pink
- White sewing cotton
- Tiny white button
- Polyester toy filling
- Thin card

For the smaller floral mushrooms

- Red and white spotty fabric, 20cm (8in) square
- White fabric, 20cm (8in) square
- Scraps of floral fabric
- Bondaweb (iron-on interfacing)
- Thin red cord, 18cm (7in) length
- Polyester toy filling
- Thin card

Finished sizes:

Large mushroom house: 14cm (5½in) square

Smaller floral mushrooms:

9.5 x 9cm (3½ x 3¾in)

Making up the large mushroom house

1 Trace the large mushroom top and stalk (see Templates) onto thin card and cut out. Place the mushroom top template onto a piece of red spotty fabric and draw around. Take another piece of fabric the same size for the back.

2 With right sides together, sew around the mushroom shape leaving a gap at the centre of the lower seam for the stalk (a). Cut out the shape and turn out to the right side. Press then stuff with polyester toy filling.

3 To make the stalk, place the large stalk template onto a piece of white fabric and draw around. Take a second piece of white fabric for the back.

4 With right sides together, sew around the stalk shape leaving a gap at the top. Cut out the shape and turn to the right side. Press then stuff with polyester toy filling. Close the gap then insert the stalk into the base of the mushroom top and stitch closed (b).

a
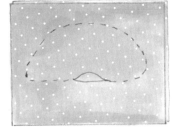

b

5 Apply Bondaweb (iron on-interfacing) onto scraps of blue, green and pink fabric. Cut out a window and door shape and place on the mushroom, as shown. Iron in place then sew around the shapes using blanket stitch and matching embroidery cotton. Add a tiny white button for the doorknob.

6 For the tiny pink flower beside the door, apply Bondaweb onto a scrap of pink fabric, cut out a tiny circle and iron onto the mushroom stalk. Sew around it with a few tiny backstitches in matching embroidery cotton and embroider a stem in backstitch using green embroidery cotton. Sew in the windowpanes using backstitch and black embroidery cotton. Finally, sew a loop of red baker's twine onto the top of the mushroom to hang.

Making up the smaller floral mushrooms

Follow Steps 1–4 for Making up the large mushroom house, using the small mushroom top and stalk templates (see Templates). To decorate, take a piece of floral fabric and apply Bondaweb onto on the back. Cut out a flower shape and iron it on to the mushroom as shown. Sew a loop of thin red cord onto the top of the mushroom to hang.

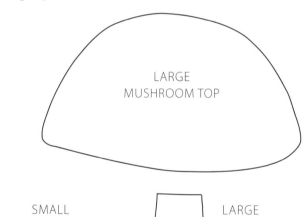

Templates

Templates shown at 50% size,
enlarge by 200%

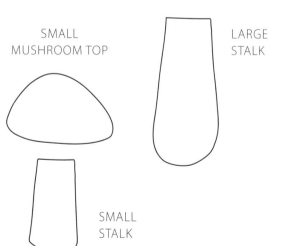

LARGE
MUSHROOM TOP

SMALL
MUSHROOM TOP

LARGE
STALK

SMALL
STALK

Merry Mouse

The perfect little festive mouse, Merry is simple to make and would look very cute beside your Christmas tree. Dress her up in traditional red and white or use your favourite festive colours and complement your colour scheme with her beautifully patterned ear lining. For a delightful finishing touch, decorate Merry's top with a dazzling snowflake brad, cute little buttons and some neat stitching. Why not use the pattern again to make a friend for Merry? They make charming Christmas gifts and will be brought out year after year.

102

You will need

For the mouse

- Cream linen, 46 x 112cm (18 x 44in)
- Scraps of red and white printed fabric
- White sewing cotton
- Black embroidery cotton
- Polyester toy filling
- Red bead
- Thin card
- Lipstick (optional)

For the clothes

- Two pieces of red felt, 20 x 10cm (8 x 4in)
- Red and white printed fabric, 10 x 32cm (4 x 12¾in) plus seam allowance
- White embroidery cotton
- Two tiny white buttons
- White snowflake brad (optional

Finished size: 30cm (12in) tall

Sewing the body

1 Trace the body, arms and legs (see Templates) onto thin card and cut out. Fold the cream linen in half and trace the card templates onto it, but do not cut out until the sewing is complete. Sew around the body, arms and legs with by machine or hand using backstitch and white sewing cotton.

2 Cut out two ears from cream linen, reversing the shape for the second one. Cut out two ear linings in the same way from red and white printed fabric and sew around them. Carefully cut out all the shapes, turn right side out and press.

3 Stuff the body with polyester toy filling and sew along the bottom with the seam facing front middle. Stuff the legs and sew to the bottom of the body with the feet facing forwards. Stuff the arms and sew to either side of the body (a).

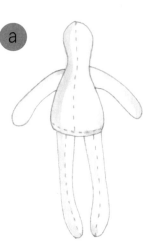

a

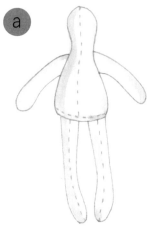

Making the clothes

1 Trace the pattern for the top (see Templates). Take two pieces of red felt and draw the pattern onto one of them. Sew up the side and sleeve seams (c).

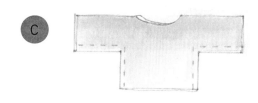

4 Sew along the bottom of the ear opening and gather (b) then sew on to the side of the head.

5 To make the face, use black embroidery cotton to sew on eyes with French knots and a mouth with backstitch. Add a red bead for the nose.

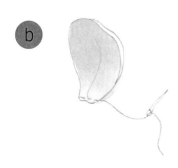

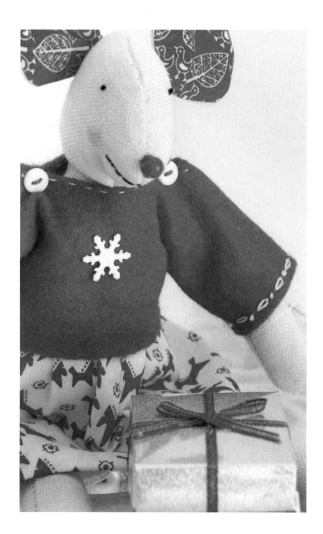

TIP To give Merry Mouse a blushing complexion, add a little lipstick to the cheeks.

2 Turn the right way out and using white embroidery cotton, sew alternate lazy daisy stitches and French knots along the cuff edges. Sew a line of running stitch around the neck. Add a tiny white button at each side of the neck to adjust the width. Fasten a snowflake brad to the front of the top for decoration.

TIP

You could use Christmas novelty fabrics for Merry Mouse's ear linings and skirt for an even more festive look.

3 To make the skirt, take the piece of red and white printed cotton and make a small hem at the bottom. Fold in the top and stitch down then sew up the back hem (d). Make small tucks around the top of the skirt until it fits the mouse shape and sew in place.

d

Merry Mouse

Templates

Templates shown at 50% size, enlarge by 200%

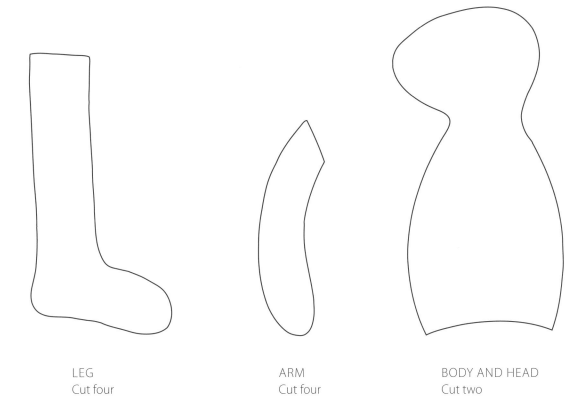

LEG
Cut four

ARM
Cut four

BODY AND HEAD
Cut two

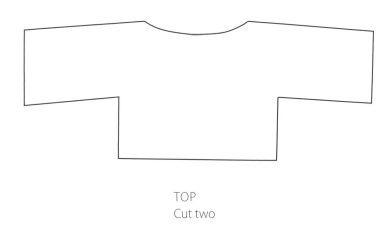

TOP
Cut two

EAR
Cut two (reversing second ear)
Cut two linings
(reversing second ear)

Sugar-free Sweets

This little collection of red and white sweets might look good enough to eat but they are sewn from fabric, so you can have as many as you like! They make delicious embellishments for a summer party or can be used to sweeten up your Christmas decorations. The lollipops are made using the paper piecing hand-sewing technique, as explained here, but they would also make a great sewing machine project. The sewn and stuffed candy canes can be tied together into scrumptious little bundles or hung individually on the Christmas tree. They look surprisingly realistic and will last much longer than the real thing!

You will need

For each lollipop

- Scraps of red fabric
- White fabric, scraps plus 8cm (3¼in) square piece for the backing
- Red and white baker's twine, 20cm (8in) length
- Scrap paper
- Lollipop stick
- Fabric glue

For each striped mint candy

- Two pieces of red and white striped fabric, 7cm (2¾in) square
- Red ric rac to tie, 30cm (12in) length
- Cellophane sweet bag

For each candy cane

- Red and white fabric, 15 x 7cm (6 x 2¾in)
- Red ric rac to tie, 30cm (12in) length

For each sugar-free sweet

- Thin card
- Polyester toy filling
- White sewing cotton

Finished sizes:

Lollipop (without stick): 8cm (3¼in) square

Striped mint candy: 7cm (2¾in) square

Candy cane: 12 x 4cm (4½ x 1½in)

Making the lollipops

1 Trace the triangle and circle shapes (see Templates) onto thin card and carefully cut out. If you are paper piecing the pinwheel blocks (see Step 2), cut out eight paper triangles using the triangle template.

2 Cut out four red and four white triangles from the fabric, giving each one a 5mm (¼in) seam allowance on each side. Tack (baste) the fabric around the paper triangles and sew them together in pairs to form a pinwheel block measuring 8cm (3¼in) square **(a)**. Snip the tacking threads and remove the papers.

3 Cut out a piece of white fabric measuring 8cm (3¼in) square for the back. Place right sides together and draw around the circle template onto the back of the pinwheel block. Sew around the shape, leaving a gap at the bottom **(b)**.

 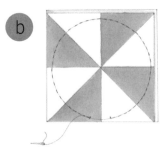

4 Cut out the circle and turn to the right side. Press then stuff with polyester toy filling. Sew up the gap at the bottom, leaving a tiny space to insert the lollipop stick. Secure the stick with a dab of fabric glue then tie a piece of red and white baker's twine in a bow at the top of the stick.

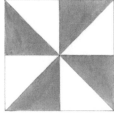

Making the striped mint candies

1 Trace the small circle (see Templates) onto thin card and cut out. Take two 7cm (2¾in) square pieces of red and white striped fabric, place right sides together and draw around the circle template onto the back of one piece. Sew around the shape before cutting out, leaving a small gap for turning.

2 Turn the circle out to the right side and press then stuff with polyester toy filling. Sew the gap closed, keeping the circle shape as even as possible.

3 Repeat Steps 1 and 2 to make six more candies. Place them all in a cellophane sweet bag and tie up the top with red ric rac.

Making the candy canes

1 Trace the candy cane (see Templates) onto a piece of thin card and cut out carefully. Take two pieces of red and white fabric and place right sides together. Draw around the candy cane template onto the back of one piece of fabric. Sew around the shape before cutting it out, leaving the base open for turning. Cut out the shape and turn to the right side.

2 Stuff with tiny pieces of polyester toy filling, using a knitting needle to help push the stuffing to the end of the candy cane. Sew up the base.

3 Repeat Steps 1 and 2 to make two more. Tie all three together in a neat bundle with red ric rac.

Templates

Templates shown at 50% size, enlarge by 200%

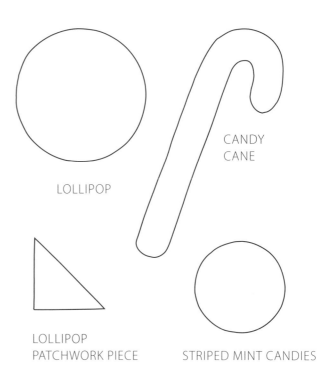

LOLLIPOP

CANDY CANE

LOLLIPOP PATCHWORK PIECE

STRIPED MINT CANDIES

Jolly Holly Stocking

Christmas stockings are delightful to make for loved ones, young and old. You cannot beat the excitement of waking up on Christmas morning to find a stocking bulging with gifts and it is even better if it has been hand-stitched with love. Stockings can be personalized and decorated in so many ways. Here I have created a charming spotty and stripy design embellished with appliqué hearts, holly and a bobble trim for a special finishing touch. I used a festive pink, red and green colour scheme but you could easily change this to blue and silver for a boy.

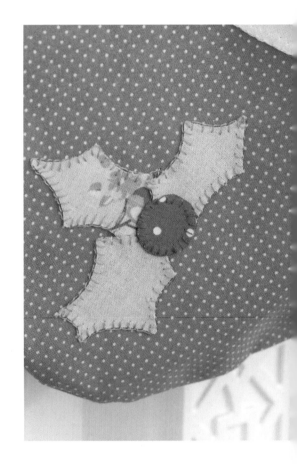

You will need

- Two pieces of red and white striped lining fabric, 58 x 31cm (22¾ x 12¼in) plus seam allowance
- Pink spotty fabric, 22 x 62cm (8½ x 24½in) plus seam allowance
- White and pink polka dot fabric, 40 x 11.5cm (16 x 4½in) plus seam allowance
- Green spotty fabric, 40 x 6.5cm (16 x 2½in) plus seam allowance
- Green floral fabric, 40 x 10.5cm (16 x 4⅛in) plus seam allowance
- Red and white striped fabric, 46 x 112cm (18 x 44in)
- Strip of white and pink polka dot fabric, 37 x 3.5cm (14½ x 1⅜in)
- Scraps of red and white spotty fabric for appliqué
- Scraps of white fabric for hearts
- Red cord, 30cm (12in) length
- Bondaweb (iron-on interfacing)
- Matching embroidery cotton
- Bobble trim in cream and red
- Red ric rac braid
- Three red heart-shaped buttons
- Thin card
- Glue gun (optional)

Finished size: 58 x 31cm (22¾ x 12¼in)

Sewing the appliqué

1 For the two sprigs of holly, apply Bondaweb (iron-on interfacing) onto scraps of green spotty and floral fabric. Transfer the templates (see Templates) onto thin card and cut out carefully. Draw around the large holly sprig template onto the green spotty fabric to make two leaves and the smaller holly sprig template onto the green floral fabric to make three leaves.

2 Apply Bondaweb onto scraps of red spotty fabric and draw around the large and small circle templates for the holly berries. Carefully cut out the leaves and berries.

3 Apply Bondaweb onto the white fabric scraps. Draw around the heart template three times on the back and cut out.

Making up the stocking leg

Jolly Holly Stocking

1 Follow the diagram **(a)** and sew together the strips of fabric starting with the red and white striped strip and continuing with the green floral strip, the second red and white striped strip, the spotty green strip and the white and pink polka dot strip. You should now have a piece of patchwork measuring 37 x 40cm (14½ x 16in) plus seam allowance.

2 Sew on the red bobble trim, the cream bobble trim and the red ric rac braid using slipstitch and matching embroidery cotton, as shown.

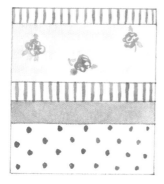

a

3 Iron on the spotty holly leaf and berry appliqué to the polka dot strip, and sew around using blanket stitch and matching embroidery cotton.

Making the stocking foot

1 Take the two pieces of pink spotty fabric and with right sides together, draw around the foot template on the back. Sew around the front curve of the foot shape, leaving the back seam open **(b)**. Trim the shape.

b

2 Turn to the right side and iron on the three white heart appliqué shapes. Sew around each one using blanket stitch and white embroidery cotton and add a heart shaped button to the centre of each appliqué heart.

3 Iron the holly leaf and berry appliqué to the toe of the stocking and sew around each shape with blanket stitch and matching embroidery cotton.

4 Take the main part of the stocking and find the centre of the bottom seam, then match to the centre of the foot section **(c)**. Pin and sew the seam.

5 With right sides together, sew up the back seam, trim the seams and turn right side out.

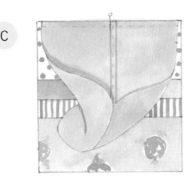

c

Making the lining and hanging loop

1 Place the two pieces of red and white striped lining fabric right sides together. Draw around the template for the foot of the stocking, adding on a 37 x 40cm (14½ x 16in) panel for the stocking leg.

2 Sew around the whole shape, leaving the top open. Trim the seams and press.

3 Place the lining inside the stocking, turn in the top then topstitch along the edge **(d)**.

d

4 For the hanging loop, fold the red cord in half and sew securely to the centre back of the stocking by hand or using a sewing machine.

5 To make the bow, fold in the strip of white and pink polka dot fabric down the long edges by 6mm (¼in), fold in half and press then top stitch right along the edge to hold in place **(e)**. Snip off the ends diagonally and tie into a bow. Attach the bow at the top of the stocking by sewing or using a glue gun.

e

Jolly Holly Stocking

Templates

Templates shown at 50% size, enlarge by 200%

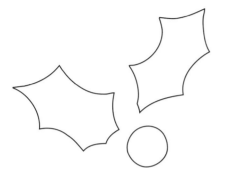

LARGE HOLLY SPRIG

SMALL HOLLY SPRIG

STOCKING FOOT

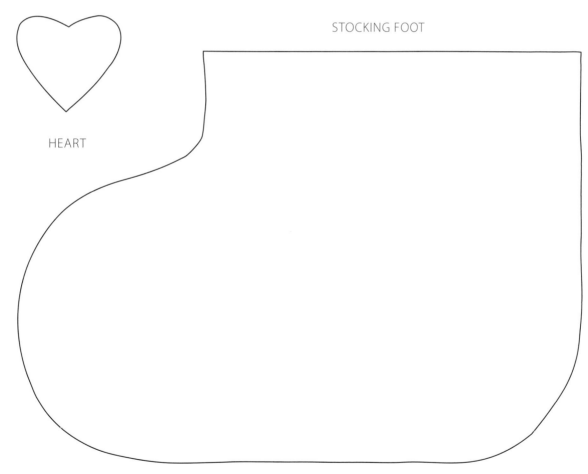

HEART

Little Deer Duo

This fun little patchwork cushion featuring a cute little appliqué deer is guaranteed to brighten up any room. The use of fresh, modern fabrics with cute buttons and trims makes this simple idea really special. You could use the basic pattern in many ways, using up your own fabric scraps and embellishments to suit your own tastes and colour schemes. If you haven't got the time to make the cushion, you might be tempted by the gorgeous little stuffed hanging decoration featuring the deer appliqué, which is so quick and simple to make.

You will need

For the Little Deer Cushion

- Turquoise spotty fabric, 9 x 24cm (3½ x 9½in) plus seam allowance
- Red berry fabric, 11.5cm (4½in) square plus seam allowance
- White fabric, 10cm (4in) square
- Smaller pieces of coordinating fabrics
- Bondaweb (iron-on interfacing)
- Cushion pad, 28 x 24cm (11 x 9½in)
- Cream bobble trim, 20cm (8in) length
- Assorted buttons
- Embroidery cotton in white and black
- Zip (optional)

For the Little Deer Hanging Decoration

- Pink and yellow spotty fabric and novelty print backing fabric, 8 x 10cm (3¼ x 4in) plus seam allowance
- Pink spotty fabric, 10cm (4in) square
- Bondaweb (iron-on interfacing)
- Cream bobble trim, 9cm (3½in) length
- Green ribbon to hang, 22cm (8½in) length
- Mother of pearl buttons
- Polyester toy filling
- Embroidery cotton in white, black and yellow

Finished sizes:

Little deer cushion: 28 x 24cm (11 x 9½in)

Hanging decoration: 8 x 10cm (3¼ x 4in)

Sewing the little deer cushion

1 Trace the little deer (see Template) onto a piece of thin card and cut out carefully. Take the white fabric square and apply Bondaweb (iron-on interfacing) onto the back. Draw around the deer template onto the back of the white fabric square, cut out then peel off the paper backing.

2 Iron the little deer appliqué shape on to the centre of the red berry patch and sew around the shape using blanket stitch and one strand of white embroidery cotton. Using black embroidery cotton, sew a nose and eyes on the deer.

3 Assemble all the patches so that you are happy with the arrangement then sew them together using a 5mm (¼in) seam. Sew on the bobble trim at the bottom of the little deer patch and add any buttons of your choice.

4 To make up the cushion, take the backing fabric and with right sides together sew around the cushion, leaving a small gap at the bottom. Turn the cushion to the right side and press. Insert the cushion pad and sew up the gap.

TIP

If you like, you can insert a zip into the bottom of the cushion for inserting the cushion pad.

2 Use two strands of yellow embroidery cotton to running stitch around the outline of the deer. Using one strand of yellow embroidery thread, sew three Algerian eye stars in the top right-hand corner.

3 Take the novelty print backing fabric and with right sides together sew right around the decoration, leaving a small gap at the bottom. Turn the decoration out the right way and press. Stuff with polyester toy filling and sew the gap closed.

4 Sew on the bobble trim, buttons and ribbon loop at the top.

Sewing the little deer hanging decoration

1 To make the appliqué deer, follow Steps 1 and 2 for Sewing the little deer cushion, using white and pink spotty fabric for the deer and pink and yellow spotty fabric for the front of the hanging decoration. Use black embroidery cotton to sew eyes and a nose onto the deer.

Template

Template shown at 50% size, enlarge by 200%

LITTLE DEER

Christmas Tree Decorations

These small stuffed Christmas trees are fun and easy to sew and can be made extra special by adding ribbons, buttons or any other decorations. I have kept to traditional festive colours but you can easily change the fabrics and embellishments to complement your own colour scheme. Raid your ribbon stash and button box and see what effects you can create. You can make just one or create a whole host of them to hang on your Christmas tree or along a string for the mantelpiece.

You will need

For each tree

- Two pieces of green fabric, 20cm (8in) square
- Three assorted pink and red ribbons
- Five assorted pink and red buttons
- Matching sewing cotton
- Polyester toy filling
- Thin pink cord, 18cm (7in) length
- Thin card

Finished size:

Each tree: 15.5 x 14cm (6⅜ x 5½in)

Sewing the tree decorations

1 Trace the Christmas tree (see Template) onto thin card and cut out carefully. Place the green fabric pieces right sides together and draw around the template onto one of them. Do not cut out until all the sewing is complete.

2 Sew around the tree shape, leaving the base open for turning. Cut out the tree shape and turn to the right side. Press then stuff firmly with polyester toy filling. Sew up the gap at the bottom of the trunk.

3 Position three lengths of assorted pink and red ribbons onto the front of the tree until you are happy with the look, then slipstitch them into place with matching sewing cotton. Sew on five different decorative buttons here and there. Finally sew a loop of thin pink cord at the top of the tree to hang.

TIP

You could also use star shaped buttons on the tree, or Christmas decoration novelty buttons.

  Christmas Tree Decorations

TIP

A nice mix of large and small, randomly placed buttons gives an interesting finish.

Template

CHRISTMAS TREE

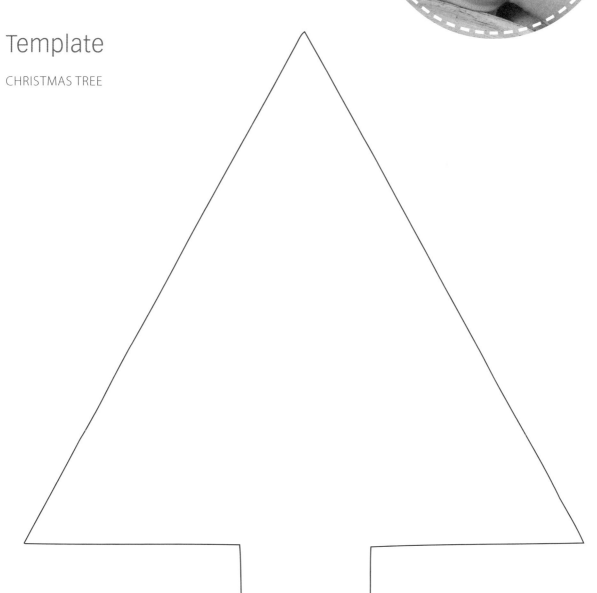

Acknowledgments

Thank you to everyone at David & Charles for their hard work, creative ideas and skill in producing this book. Thank you to Katy Denny for commissioning the book, for all her ideas and inspiration, and for being so wonderfully organized. Thank you to my Project Editor, Beth Dymond, and Editors, James Brooks and Grace Harvey for all their hard work, help and assistance.

A big thank you to Victoria Marks for her fabulous book design and styling, and of course a special thank you to Simon Whitmore for the gorgeous photography and for making the book look beautiful. Finally, thank you as always to my wonderful husband David and my lovely family for all their love and support.

About the Author

Helen Philipps studied printed textiles and embroidery at Manchester Metropolitan University and then taught drawing and design before becoming a freelance designer. After working in the greetings card industry, Helen's love of needlecraft led her to create original designs for stitching magazines and books. Her work features regularly in many stitch and craft magazines and she also writes a popular craft blog: **helenphilipps.blogspot.co.uk.**

This is Helen's eighth book for David and Charles, following on from *Simple Sewn Gifts* published in 2010.

Suppliers

- **Fabric Rehab:** www.fabricrehab.co.uk

- **Fancy Moon:** www.fancymoon.co.uk

- **The Fat Quarter Shop:** www.fatquartershop.com

- **Fred Aldous:** www.fredaldous.co.uk
  for tape measure ribbon and many crafts supplies

- **Hobbycraft Stores:** www.hobbycraft.co.uk
  for many crafts supplies

- **Quilter's Cloth:** www.quilterscloth.co.uk

- **Stitch Craft Create:** www.stitchcraftcreate.co.uk

- **Sew and So:** www.sewandso.co.uk
  for pastel linen, Just Another Button Company buttons (used for the birds in the Lollipop Flowers Picture), DMC threads and a huge range of sewing products

- **The Stamp Attic:** www.thestampattic.co.uk
  for Tim Holz Haberdashery rubber stamps

Index

A DAVID & CHARLES BOOK
© F&W Media International, Ltd 2013

David & Charles is an imprint of F&W Media International, Ltd
Brunel House, Forde Close, Newton Abbot, TQ12 4PU, UK

F&W Media International, Ltd is a subsidiary of F+W Media, Inc
10151 Carver Road, Suite #200, Blue Ash, OH 45242, USA

Text and Designs © Helen Philipps 2013
Layout and Photography © F&W Media International, Ltd 2013

First published in the UK and USA in 2013

A catalogue record for this book is available from the British Library.

ISBN-13: 978-1-4463-0213-2 paperback
ISBN-10: 1-4463-0213-X paperback

Printed in China by RR Donnelley for:
F&W Media International, Ltd
Brunel House, Forde Close, Newton Abbot, TQ12 4PU, UK

10 9 8 7 6 5 4 3 2 1

Senior Acquisitions Editor: Katy Denny
Junior Acquisitions Editor: James Brooks
Assistant Editor: Grace Harvey
Project Editor: Beth Dymond
Senior Designer: Victoria Marks
Photographer: Simon Whitmore
Senior Production Controller: Kelly Smith

F+W Media publishes high quality books on a wide range of subjects.
For more great book ideas visit: www.stitchcraftcreate.co.uk